Internet safety

You'll have access to millions of pages of information when you're exploring the Internet, but not all Web sites will be as good as the ones recommended in this book. You may come into contact with some unpleasant and potentially dangerous sites, or even people. To ensure you stay safe when you're online, make sure you follow these guidelines:

- Never arrange to meet anyone you get to know over the Internet.
- If you write a message in a chat room, or on a Web site message board, do not include your e-mail address or any other personal information, such as your real name, address or telephone number.
- If you reach a site containing anything unpleasant, hit your browser's *Stop* button to stop downloading it, then the *Back* button to return to the previous page. (See page 8.)

Before you start any of the projects in this book, turn to page 60 and read the detailed Internet safety guide. You'll also find extra safety tips in boxes throughout the book.

Getting started

If you're new to the Internet, pages 4-7 explain what it is, and how to get online. Once you're connected, you can turn to page 8 and start the projects. Most of the projects use programs which you'll already have on your computer.

The instructions in this book are aimed at personal computer users with *Microsoft® Windows® 98*, or a later version. It doesn't matter if you don't have exactly the same programs. Most programs of the same type work in a similar way, although the commands may be slightly different.

You may need to download some extra free programs to complete some of the projects in this book. If you do, you'll find instructions about how and where to get them outlined in the project.

What is the Internet?

The Internet is a huge computer network linking together millions of smaller networks all over the world. When you connect to the Internet you are "online". You will have access to millions of pages of information, as well as lots of useful services, and you will be able to communicate with people across the world.

More and more people are connecting to the Internet each month. Lots of people use it everyday for work, school and leisure. You can do research on it, go shopping, get the latest news reports, play games, and chat to people using e-mail (electronic mail). This book will show you how to do all these things and more. The pictures on these two pages show just a few of the sites and services available to you.

Lots of schools and colleges have their own Web sites. The Internet is a great educational resource.

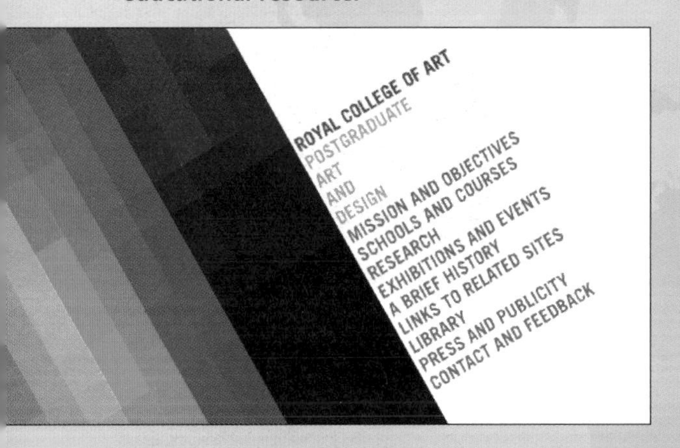

You can shop for just about anything; music, books, clothes, food...

The World Wide Web

The World Wide Web, also known as the Web, contains millions of documents called Web pages. These pages can include text, still and moving pictures, and sound.

Most organizations on the World Wide Web have sets of pages which are linked together. These sets of pages are called Web sites. The Web is the fastest-growing part of the Internet, with hundreds of new pages appearing each day. You can use it to get up-to-date information about almost any subject.

Every Web page has its own address, called a URL (Uniform Resource Locator). This makes it easy to find pages and to return to pages you've visited before.

This is an example URL:

http://www.usborne.com/home.html

- ***http://*** — This tells you that the page is a Web page.
- ***www.usborne.com*** — This tells you the name of the computer on which the page is kept.
- ***home.html*** — This tells the computer the filename of the page.

This URL tells your computer that the page is called *home.html*, and that it is stored on a computer at *www.usborne.com*.

There are thousands of games to play on the Internet.

Online communication

As well as reading Web pages over the Internet, you can also use it to communicate with other Internet users through e-mail. You can send a message to someone, no matter where they are in the world, and it will reach them in a matter of seconds. It only costs the price of a local telephone call to send and receive messages. You'll find more about e-mail on pages 14-15 and other forms of Internet communication on pages 16-17.

E-mail is a fun and easy way to stay in touch with friends and family.

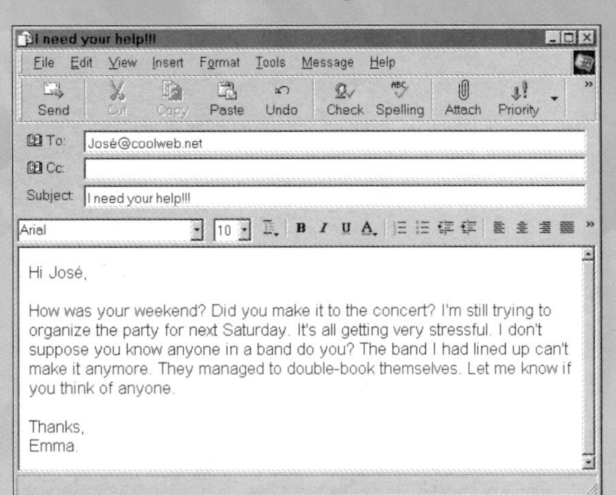
I need your help!!!

File Edit View Insert Format Tools Message Help

Send Cut Copy Paste Undo Check Spelling Attach Priority

To: José@coolweb.net

Cc:

Subject: I need your help!!!

Hi José,

How was your weekend? Did you make it to the concert? I'm still trying to organize the party for next Saturday. It's all getting very stressful. I don't suppose you know anyone in a band do you? The band I had lined up can't make it anymore. They managed to double-book themselves. Let me know if you think of anyone.

Thanks,
Emma.

There are museum sites on everything from dinosaurs and space, to music and art.

Internet services

The Internet has lots of useful services and this book will show you how to make the most of them. You can get up-to-the-minute news and weather reports, as well as the latest sport scores. You can shop for just about anything, use train and plane timetables, and find out about the latest film and music releases.

You can keep up-to-date on the latest movie releases, watch previews online, or go behind the scenes.

You can get a weather forecast for anywhere in the world in an instant.

Getting online

To use the Internet, you need a computer, a modem and a telephone line. You will also have to sign up with an Internet Service Provider (ISP) to get connected to the Internet.

What type of computer?

You don't have to have a high-powered computer to get online. Computer memory and storage space is measured in megabytes (MB). You need at least 32MB of RAM to use Internet and Web software. (RAM stands for "Random Access Memory" and is the part of your computer which enables it to use programs.)

Software and information you want to keep permanently is stored on your computer's hard disk. You'll need at least 200MB of free hard disk space to store Internet software.

What is a modem?

A modem is a device which enables computers to communicate with each other via telephone lines. The modem translates computer information into telephone signals, so it can be carried across the Internet, and then converts it back into computer information again.

There are two types of modems that can be used with desktop computers: internal modems and external modems. An internal modem fits inside your computer's processing unit. Most new personal computers come with one already fitted. An external modem connects to your computer by a cable which plugs into a socket, called a serial port, at the back of your computer.

Modems transfer data to and from the Internet at different speeds. The speed is measured in bits per second (bps). It is a good idea to use a modem which works at a speed of 56,000 bps (56Kbps or 56K). The faster your modem works, the less time you will spend waiting for Web pages to download onto your computer, which can be frustrating.

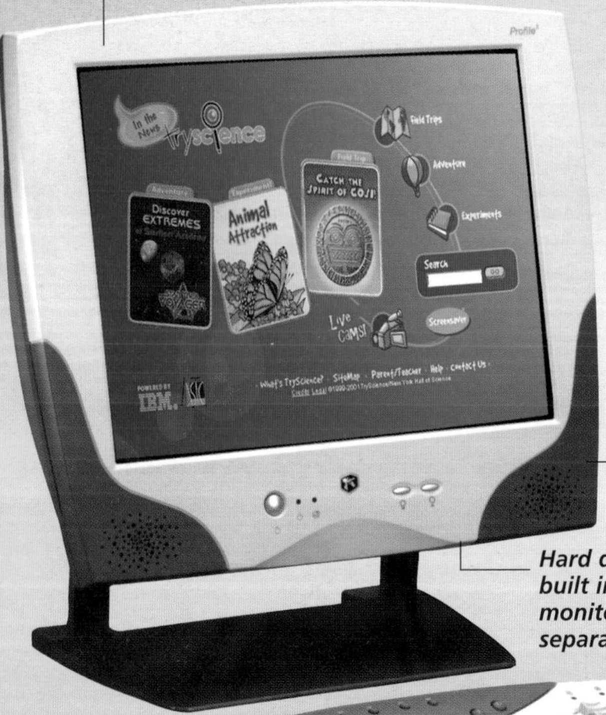

Monitor

Speakers ~ these are sometimes separate units.

Hard drive ~ this one is built into the back of the monitor. Some come as a separate unit.

An inkjet (or bubblejet) printer ~ these are fairly inexpensive and ideal for home use.

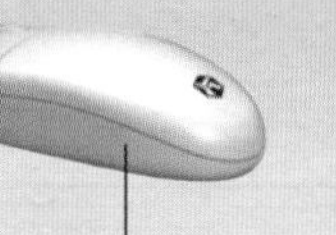

Mouse

Keyboard

Will I need any extra equipment?

To complete some of the projects in this book you may need some extra equipment.

To print Web pages, pictures or text, you'll need a printer. Alternatively you could take a floppy disk containing documents to a printing store that can print them for you.

If you have a multimedia computer, it will probably be equipped with speakers and a sound card, so that you will be able to hear music and video clips, or other sounds over the Internet. If you don't want to disturb other people, you could use headphones instead of speakers.

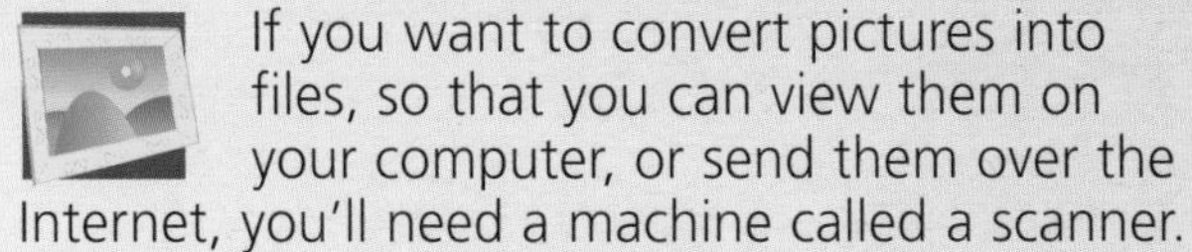

If you want to convert pictures into files, so that you can view them on your computer, or send them over the Internet, you'll need a machine called a scanner.

A scanner divides pictures into tiny dots known as pixels. It records information about each pixel and stores all the information it collects as a computer file. You use "imaging" software (which comes with the scanner) to tell it how many pixels to divide a picture into.

If you don't have access to a scanner, companies that develop photographs will scan pictures for you. Alternatively, a digital camera stores photographs as computer files which you can copy onto your computer (see page 26).

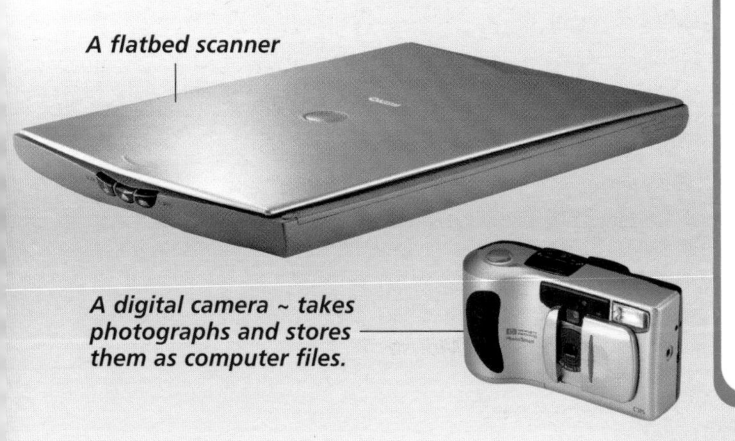

A flatbed scanner

A digital camera ~ takes photographs and stores them as computer files.

Internet Service Providers

To connect your computer to the Internet you'll need to sign up with a company called an Internet Service Provider (ISP). You connect to an ISP through your modem and telephone line, then the ISP connects you to the Internet. Some well-known ISPs are *AOL*, *MSN* and *Virgin.net*.

There are hundreds of ISPs to choose from. Each has its own set of services and charges. Some charge a small monthly fee for using their services and you also have to pay for the time you spend online (this is charged at local call rate). Other ISPs charge nothing for their services, but you still have to pay your telephone company for the time you spend online. Some ISPs charge a fixed monthly fee, which allows you unlimited time online at no extra charge.

Finding the right ISP for you depends on how long you want to spend online and how much support you need. Ask friends if they can recommend one, or look through an Internet magazine, such as *the net* or *Internet Magazine*, for ISP advertisements. These should include details about what services they offer and where you can contact them.

Once you have selected an ISP, they will send you instructions about how to set up your equipment, as well as the software you need to get online, and instructions on how to install it on your computer.

Before you start

As you do the projects in this book, you'll produce new files on your computer. It's a good idea to create a folder on your computer's desktop, to store all the documents you make using this book. This will make it easy to find everything later.

Close any programs you have open and right click on the desktop. From the menu that appears, select *New*. Another menu should appear. Now, click on *Folder*, and a new yellow folder should pop up as an icon on your desktop. Type in the name *Projects*.

Using a browser

A browser is the program which you use to look at Web pages. The two most frequently used browsers are *Microsoft® Internet Explorer* (shown here), which comes free with *Microsoft® Windows® 98*, and *Netscape® Navigator.* They both work in a similar way.

The Web page is displayed here.

The Microsoft® Internet Explorer *browser window*

Use the Back button to see the last page you looked at.

Type in a site's address here.

This button reloads the most up-to-date version of a page.

This displays a list of all the sites you have visited today.

This is the title of the Web page and the browser you're using.

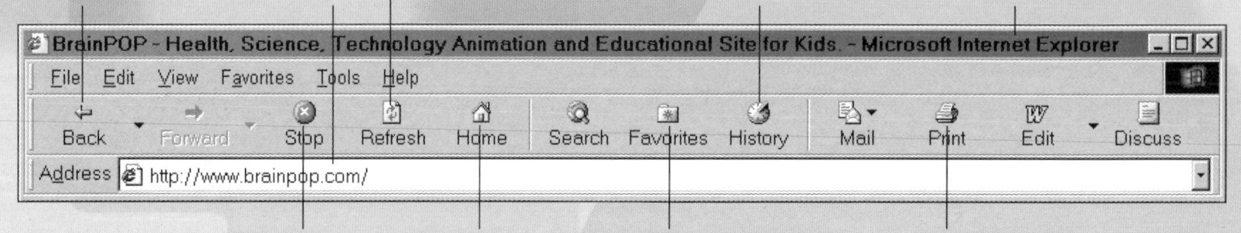

Use the Stop button if you decide you no longer want to download a particular page.

This button returns you to your home page.

You can store a list of the sites you visit most often here.

Hit this button to print the Web page you're on.

1 • Go to a Web page

The easiest way to find a Web page is to type its address into your browser's *Address* or *Location* box. Connect to the Internet and start up your browser. Click in the *Address* box and delete the URL if there is one showing. Type in the URL of a Web site and press *Return*. Your browser will download the Web site's entry page, which is known as its home page.

This is the home page of the film Shrek.

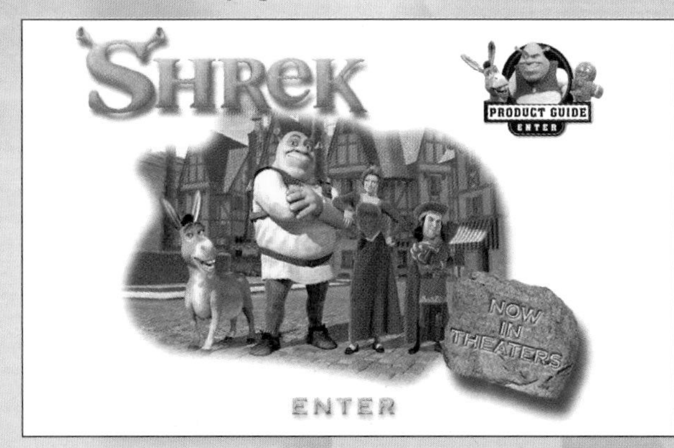

2 • Short cut to a Web page

When you find a Web page you like, you can create a short cut in your browser, so you can find it again quickly. These short cuts are called "Favorites" in *Microsoft® Internet Explorer*", and "Bookmarks" in *Netscape® Navigator.* They're useful because URLs are not easy to remember. It's a good idea to create a short cut whenever you find a page you like. This makes it easier to remember sites and visit them again later.

To create a short cut in *Netscape Navigator,* download your chosen page, go to *Bookmarks* on your menu bar, and select *Add Bookmark.* To look at the Web page you've bookmarked, simply click on its name from the *Bookmarks* menu while you are connected to the Internet.

To create a short cut in *Microsoft Internet Explorer*, download the page and select *Add to Favorites* from the *Favorites* menu. To view the Web page later, click on its name from the *Favorites* menu while you are online.

Searching online

For links to the Web sites featured in these projects, go to www.usborne-quicklinks.com and type the keywords "101 Internet".

There are so many pages and sites on the Internet that it's easy to feel swamped with information. The best way to find pages with specific information is by using a program called a search engine. There are two types of search engine. One looks for Web pages that contain particular words. This type is called an index. The other kind, called a directory, breaks down Web sites into categories and lists sites in each one. This type is useful for more general searching.

Search engines are compiled by teams of editors, or by computers which sift through, and categorize, Web sites. Because there is so much material being added to the Internet all the time, no search engine can list every Web site. When you are looking for information on a particular subject, it's a good idea to use at least two different search engines, to ensure you get a selection of relevant pages. Some tell you about new, interesting, or popular sites and others have their own news and weather pages.

Indexes

Google puts its search findings in order of relevance.

AltaVista® and HotBot® have very large databases to search.

Directories

Yahoo!® has lots of other useful services.

You can type in a question at Ask Jeeves™.

KidsClick! and Yahooligans! are great for kids.

3 • Carry out a keyword search

You can search the Internet by typing keywords into a search engine, such as **Google**. A keyword is a word which sums up the subject of a page, or which appears a number of times on it.

On the Google search page you will see a box where you can type in your keyword. This is called a query box. Try typing the keyword **chimpanzee** into the query box. Next, click on the *Google Search* button.

The search engine will compile a list of Web pages which contain that keyword, and the results are then presented as a list of links. At the top of the list you'll see the number of results. You can click on any link to visit one of the Web pages.

A search using Google

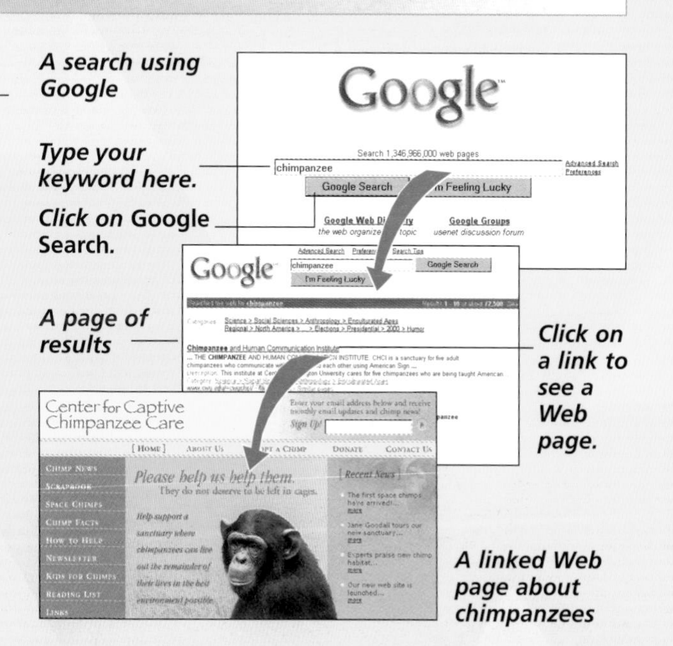

Type your keyword here.

Click on Google Search.

A page of results

Click on a link to see a Web page.

A linked Web page about chimpanzees

4 • Search by category

When you do a search using a directory, such as **Yahooligans!**, you gradually narrow down the subject area of the page you're looking for.

If, for example, you want to see a page about a television show, start by clicking on *Arts and Entertainment* on the Yahooligans! home page. A page of *Arts and Entertainment* sub-categories will download. Select *Television* and, from the page which downloads, select *Shows*.

Scroll down the next page, which contains a list of television show sites, and click on the title of the show you are looking for. If there is only one site in the directory to link to for this show, you will be taken directly to it. If there are several related sites, you will be taken to another page where you can select one.

5 • Visit a portal

Search engines and directories aren't the only way of finding information. You could also try visiting a portal. A portal is a site which has lots of links to other sites. As search engine sites have lots of links, they are technically considered to be portals, but there are also some very specialized Web sites, which have links to useful sites on a particular subject.

For example, the **CinemaSpot Web site** is a movie portal. It has links to hundreds of useful film-related sites. If you were trying to find information on a particular movie, you might find it much more quickly by visiting CinemaSpot, rather than by using the Yahooligans! directory.

CinemaSpot is part of the **StartSpot Network**, which is a collection of useful portals. These include the **TripSpot Web site**, which has links to the best travel sites, and the **HomeworkSpot site**, which is great for homework help. Each portal guides you through the best sites and makes it easy to find what you're looking for. Visit the StartSpot Network home page, and choose a portal from there.

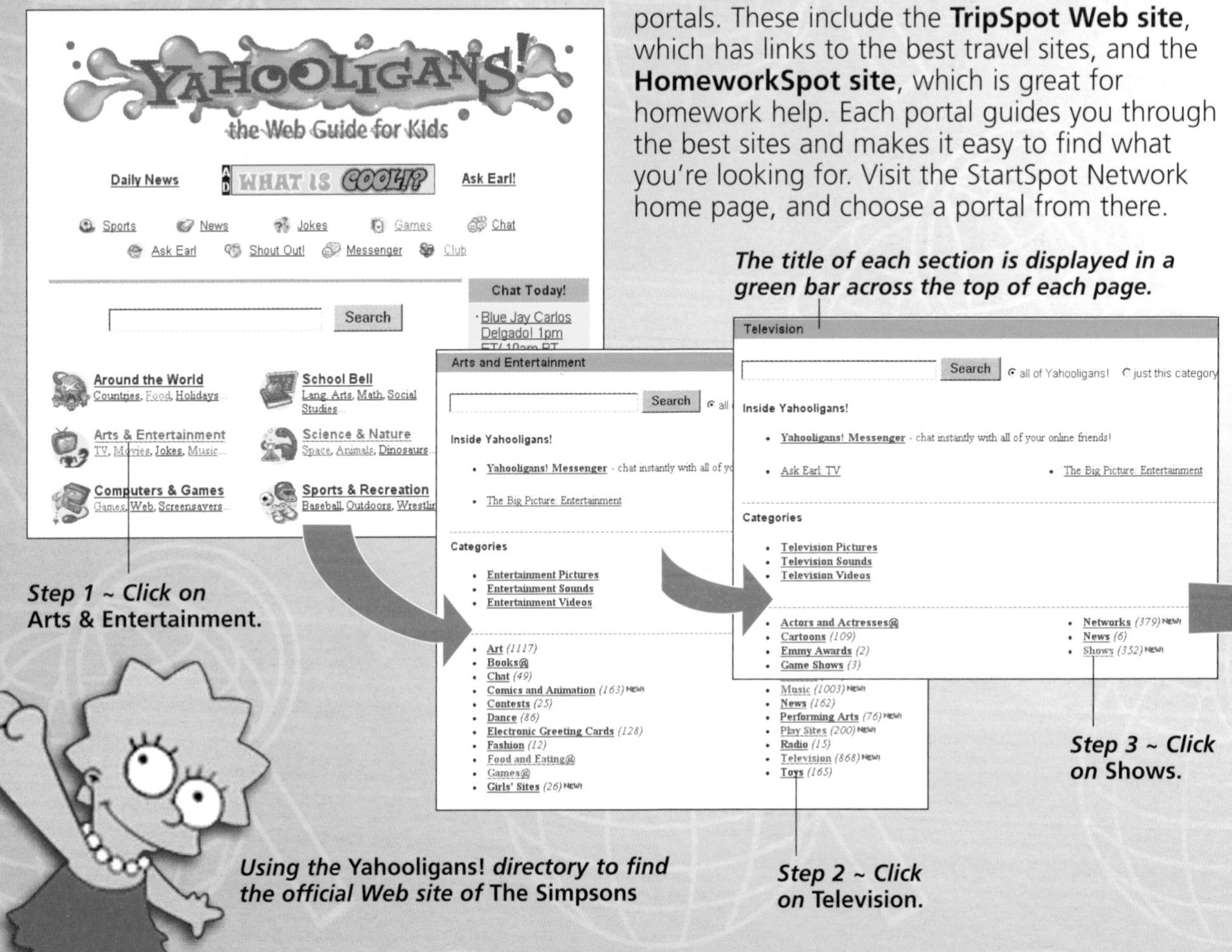

The title of each section is displayed in a green bar across the top of each page.

Step 1 ~ Click on **Arts & Entertainment.**

Step 2 ~ Click on **Television.**

Step 3 ~ Click on **Shows.**

Using the **Yahooligans!** ***directory to find the official Web site of*** **The Simpsons**

6 • Do an advanced search

Sometimes a search using only one keyword can produce thousands of results and it is difficult to know where to get started. If this happens, you can narrow down your search by doing an "advanced search". One of the best search engines for doing very detailed searches is the **AltaVista® Web site**.

A common method of performing an advanced search is to look for a specific name or phrase on a Web page. To do this, you put quotation marks around the words. For example, to look for a Web page about a band called New Sound, you would type in **"New Sound"**.

If you want to find a Web page featuring several words which don't necessarily appear together, put a **+** sign in front of each keyword. For example, you could find a page about the vaccinations you need if you are going to Indonesia by typing in **+vaccinations +Indonesia**.

You can use similar methods to exclude pages. So, if you want to search for a Web page about travel vaccinations, but you don't want information about rabies, use the **-** sign, as in **+vaccinations -rabies**.

***An advanced search using* AltaVista®**

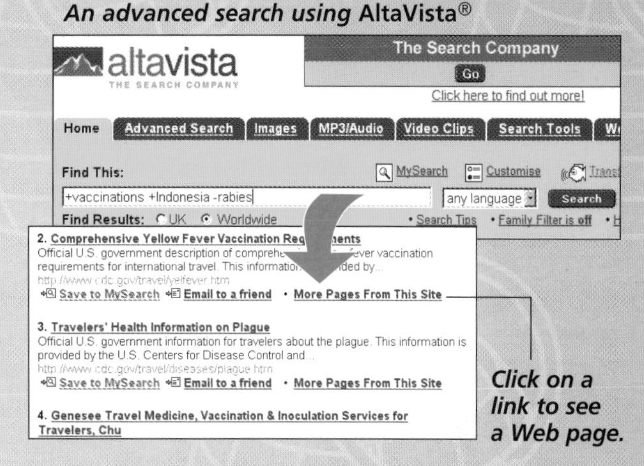

Click on a link to see a Web page.

Changing Web addresses

Because the Internet is developing so quickly, it is common for URLs to change. You may find that when you revisit a site, you reach a page that says the site can't be found or reached at that moment. First, try checking the site again later. If you still can't access it, it may have moved to a new address. Try using a search engine to find it, or a similar site. Search using the name of the site, or a suitable keyword.

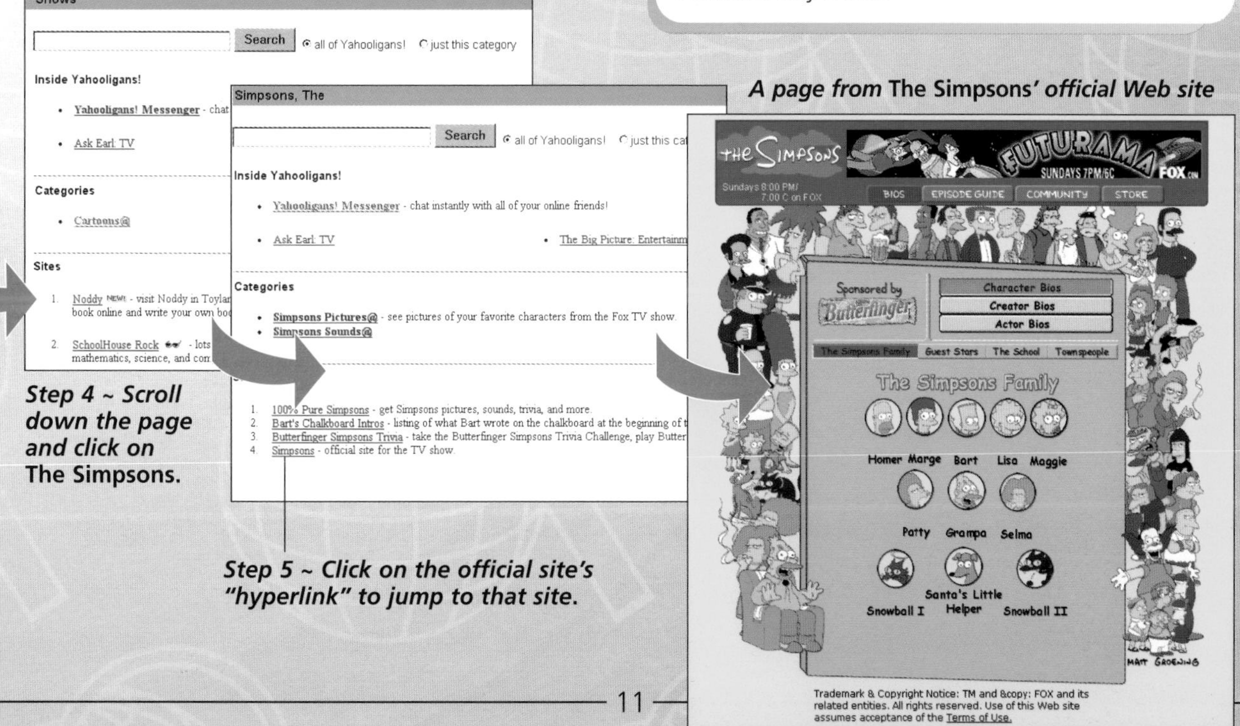

***Step 4 ~ Scroll down the page and click on* The Simpsons.**

Step 5 ~ Click on the official site's "hyperlink" to jump to that site.

A page from* The Simpsons' *official Web site

Downloading programs

There is a huge range of programs to download on the Internet. Lots of the projects in this book involve downloading programs which you can use to play games, watch film trailers and listen to music clips. Here you'll find advice on downloading, installing and unzipping them.

7 • Download a plug-in

A "plug-in" is a program that you can add to your browser, which enables it to show special features on Web pages, such as video clips, interactive games or animations. If a Web page has been created using a plug-in that you don't have, you'll usually see a link to a site where you can download it.

RealPlayer® is a plug-in which enables you to play sound and video clips on Web sites. You can download it at the **Real.com Web site**.

The* RealPlayer® *screen

From the home page, select your language from the drop-down menu, and click on *RealPlayer*. Make sure you select the version which says *'our free player'* beside it.

Fill in the online form, providing your e-mail address and information about your computer system. (This will ensure that you download the most suitable version of the program for your computer.) When you have completed the form, click on *Download FREE RealPlayer*.

You will see a page with links to sites around the world. Select the link to the site geographically nearest to you, and click *download*. You'll see a *File Download* window.

Security warnings

Sometimes when you are downloading programs, or trying to send information across the Internet, your browser may display a window warning you that the information is not secure. This means it could be seen by somebody else. If you follow the safety guidelines throughout this book, it will be safe for you just to click *OK* in this window.

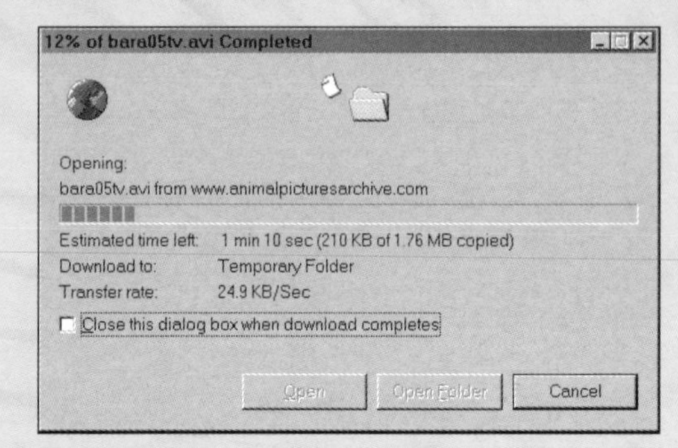

The* File Download *window

Select *Save this program to disk,* and click on *OK*. A *Save As* window will appear. Browse through the folders on your C drive, and select the *Temp* folder as the save destination. This file should appear with the main ones on your C drive, such as *System* and *Programs*.

A new *File Download* window will appear. This tells you the name of the program file and gives you an estimate of how much time it will take to download. A *Download complete* window will appear when the program has been downloaded successfully. Use project 8 to install *RealPlayer®* on your computer.

Different programs

There are lots of different ways of installing programs, so the instructions on these pages may not work for every program that you download. You'll usually find full installation instructions for a particular program on the Web site that features it, or in a *Help* or *Read Me* file that downloads at the same time as the program files.

8 • Install a plug-in

Once you have downloaded a program from the Internet, you have to install it before you can use it. A program such as *RealPlayer®* (see project 7) will usually install itself automatically on your computer, if you carry out the following instructions.

Make sure you are offline (not connected to the Internet) and your browser is closed. Open *Windows® Explorer.* (Click on *Start* and then *Programs* to find it.) Then, look for the *Temp* folder where you saved the *RealPlayer* program file. Double-click on this to start the installation process.

You will see a *Setup* screen, giving instructions on how to install *RealPlayer®*. Click on *Next* after you have read each screen. An *Installation* screen will appear. This will tell you where the *RealPlayer* program will be installed on your C drive. This is usually a folder called **C:\Program Files\Real\Player** or **C:\Real\Player**. Click *Next* to continue.

On the next page, you'll be given lots of installation options. Make sure you tick *'Add a desktop short cut to RealPlayer',* as this will make it easy to find. (The other options aren't important.) Click *Continue* to finish the installation. Finally, you need to complete an online registration form. Enter your e-mail address, country and postcode, and then choose your personalized settings for *RealPlayer*. When this is complete, click *Finish.* You can now access *RealPlayer* by clicking on the desktop icon.

© Phong for Bechamel

9 • Unzip a program

A lot of the programs you download will be in the form of "zip" files. These are files that have been compressed, so they take up less space when stored on a computer's hard disk. They can also be sent across the Internet more quickly. Zip files have filenames ending in *.zip*.

One place where you will come across zip files is the **Games Domain site**, where you can download lots of games. When you find a game you would like to try out, use the method described in project 7 to download its file.

Before you can use a program that has been zipped, you need to decompress, or "unzip", it. If you own a PC, you will need a program called *WinZip®* (which you can download from the **WinZip Web site**). If you use an Apple Mac, you can download a similar program called *StuffIt* at the **Aladdin Systems Web site**.

To unzip a zip file with *WinZip 8.0*, first Open *WinZip*. You'll see a "license agreement" window. To use the program, click *I Agree*. The *WinZip Wizard* window, shown here, may appear on screen. (If it doesn't, select *Wizard...* from the *File* menu in the window that appears.)

WinZip Wizard will guide you through the process of unzipping the program and installing it on your computer. During this process, you'll see a list of zip files stored on your computer. You'll need to select the name of the zipped file you downloaded. *WinZip Wizard* will tell you where it will store the program on your computer when it has finished. It usually unzips programs into a folder called **C:\Unzipped**.

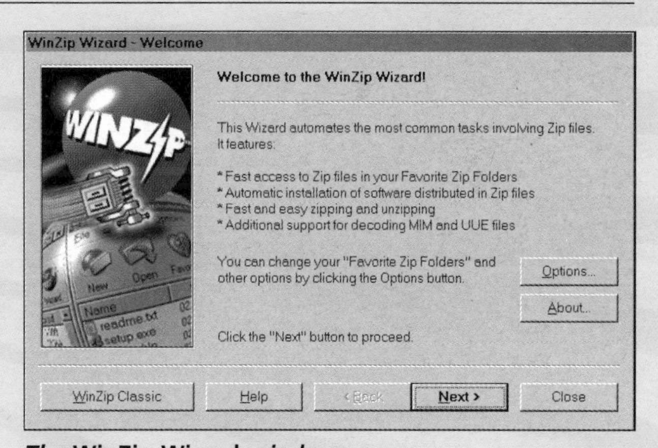

The **WinZip Wizard** *window*

When you want to play the game, use *Windows® Explorer* to find this folder, and look for a filename ending in *.exe.* Double-click on this filename to start the game.

Exploring e-mail

E-mail is one of the most popular features of the Internet. It's a great way to keep in touch with people. The projects here will help you to get started.

The projects in this section use *Microsoft® Outlook® Express*, the free e-mail program that comes with *Microsoft® Windows 98*. You will find that most other e-mail programs work in a similar way, although the commands may be slightly different.

10 • Send an e-mail

Everyone who is connected to the Internet has an e-mail address. This identifies where their messages will be sent to. Here is an imaginary e-mail address:

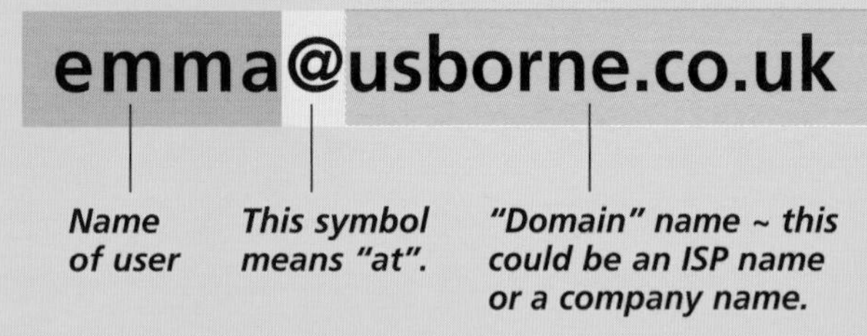

E-mail is very quick and cheap to use, because sending a message only costs the same as a local phone call and usually takes just a couple of minutes to reach its destination. To send an e-mail, open your e-mail program. A window similar to the one shown below will appear:

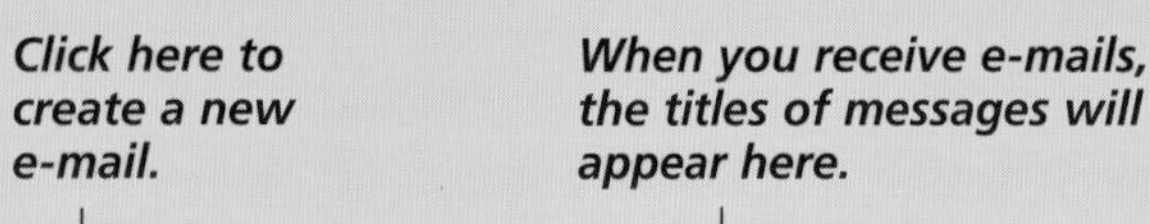

Click here to create a new e-mail.

When you receive e-mails, the titles of messages will appear here.

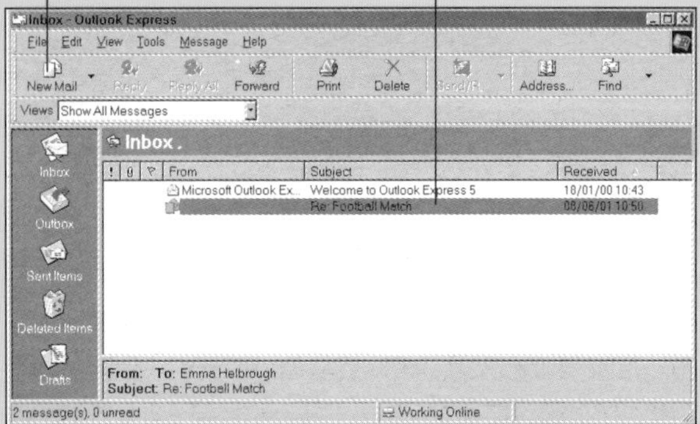

The **Microsoft® Outlook® Express** ***window***

Click on the *New Mail* button to create a new message. A window like the one shown below will appear. Click in the *To:* box, and type in the e-mail address of the person you're sending it to. Click in the main box and type your message. Think of a title for the e-mail and type it in the *Subject* box. Go online and click on the *Send* button to send the message.

Click here to send the e-mail while you are online. ***Type the address in here.*** ***Give the message a title.*** ***Type your message in here.***

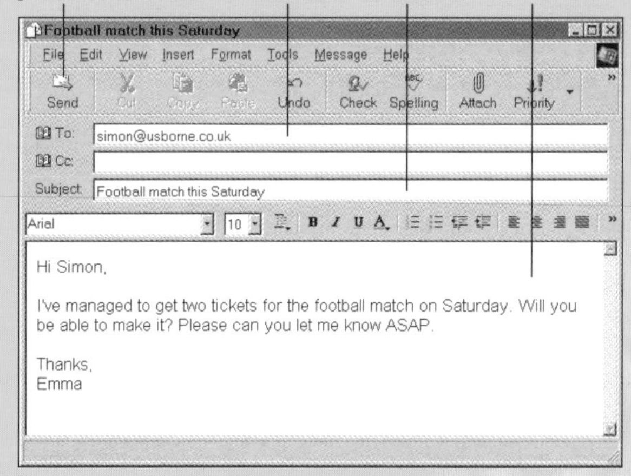

Microsoft® Outlook® Express ***composition window***

11 • Join a mailing list

A mailing list is a group of people who communicate with each other via e-mail. Each group has an official e-mail address, and when someone sends a message to that address it is forwarded to every member on the list.

Mailing lists are used by enthusiasts to exchange messages about a hobby, sport or other interest. They are also a good way of keeping in contact with old friends from school, or work. You could try doing a keyword search (see project 3) to find a mailing list to suit you. Use the name of your personal interest as a keyword and add **+"mailing list"**.

To join a mailing list, you usually have to send an e-mail with the word *subscribe* in the title to a given address. When you join, you will usually be sent a message with all the essential information about the list.

12 • Send an animated message

Why not brighten up someone's day with an animated e-mail message, or "e-card"? It could be for a birthday, to wish someone good luck, or you might just want to say "hi". The **Blue Mountain Web site** has some fun animated e-cards. From the home page, click on a category, such as *Birthdays*. Then, click on a thumbnail (small picture) to see an animation.

When you find an animated picture you like, click on *Personalize and send this card.* You may be asked if you want to send a gift with it. Click on *Continue* at the top of the page to send a free card without a gift. Fill in the online form, and click *Continue.* When the person receives the e-mail, it will contain a link to a Web page where they can see the e-card.

***An animated e-card from the* Blue Mountain Web site**

13 • Design an e-mail signature

In some e-mail programs, you can make your messages more personal by adding a special signature to them. This could be a picture made from letters and numbers, or it could include a quotation or joke.

It's easy to add an e-mail signature to your messages in *Microsoft® Outlook® Express*. Click on *Tools* on the menu bar, followed by *AutoSignature*. A dialog box will be displayed and you can type in your signature design. This will automatically be saved to use in the future.

If you would like it to appear at the end of every message you send, select *Add this signature to the end of new messages.* Alternatively, you can add it selectively, by clicking on *Insert* then *AutoSignature* at the end of individual messages.

An e-mail signature can combine pictures and words.

```
            Drop me
            a line...
        O  o
   _\    o
\\/ O\
//\ __ =
    /
```

```
 ,-.____,-.
 \ /)  "  (\ /
  (__O__)
  /      \/)
 ( || || )
  000.000
Paws and e-mail me!
```

Safety

If you choose to add your e-mail signature automatically at the end of every message, be careful what information you include in it. Don't include your address, telephone number, or any other personal information.

The Internet makes staying in touch with family and friends easy, no matter how far away they live. You can chat to someone on the other side of the world, or just discuss what to do this evening with a friend around the corner.

14 • Use a Messenger program

There are lots of different ways to chat on the Internet, but you should always approach them with caution. Although it can be a great way of meeting new friends, it is equally easy to meet some unpleasant characters.

Try to use safer forms of online chatting, such as *Yahooligans! Messenger*. This is a free chat program, used by people of all ages, which you can download at the **Yahooligans! Web site**.

There are lots of Messenger programs available to download but, unlike others, *Yahooligans! Messenger* only allows you to receive messages from people who you have added to your "friends" address list. This means you won't get any unwanted visitors trying to contact you. Another unique feature is that you can customize the look of your program with themes, such as "sports" and "happy".

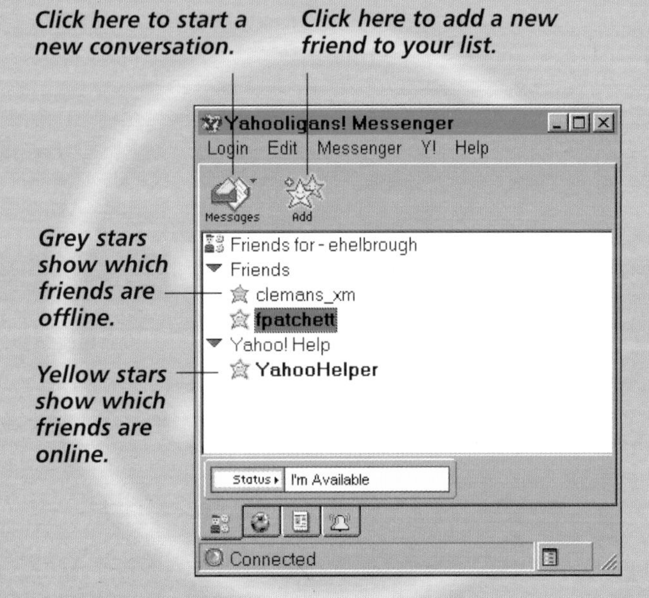

The Yahooligans! Messenger *window*

Unlike e-mails, *Yahooligans! Messenger* works in "real-time", which means that chat is spontaneous. You can reply to each other instantly and the whole conversation is displayed on screen, sentence-by-sentence. You can also have more than two people chatting at once, and you can tell which of your friends are online when you are connected.

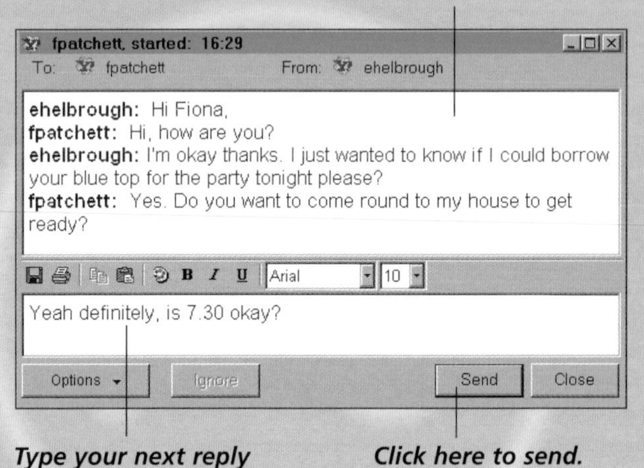

The Yahooligans! Messenger *chat window*

To download the program, click on *Messenger* on the Yahooligans! home page, and select *Get it now.* Follow the instructions on the next page to install the program. (You can save it in your desktop "*Projects*" folder: see page 7 for help.) In order to register, you have to sign up for a Yahoo! ID. If you're under 18, you'll need your parents', or guardians', permission.

Safe chatting

- Don't continue talking to people who say things you don't like.
- Never give out any personal details to people you have met over the Internet.
- Be aware that people can pretend to be whoever they like when they chat online.
- Never arrange to meet anyone you get to know over the Internet.

15 • Create your own mailing list

Mailing lists can by used as a form of online chat between friends, although they aren't as spontaneous as Messenger programs.

At the **Yahoo! Groups Web site**, you can create a private mailing list, which only includes your circle of friends. At the site, you'll find easy-to-follow instructions on how to start a list, and how to run it. Click on *Start a new Group!* on the home page, and fill in the online form.

In order to circulate messages, you need to create a group e-mail address, which will forward messages to all members. At Yahoo! Groups, all e-mail addresses end with: *@yahoogroups.com,* so you just have to select a group name to prefix this. If, for example, your mailing list was about sharing recipes, you could call your group name: *cool_recipes* and your e-mail address would be: *cool_recipes@ yahoogroups.com.*

If you want to keep your mailing list private, make sure you select *Unlisted,* so that your group will not be displayed in the Yahoo! Groups directory, and *Closed,* so that only you can invite new members to join. You'll find lots of helpful advice and a list of answers to Frequently Asked Questions (FAQs) by clicking on *Check out Help* on the Yahoo! Groups home page.

Mailing list tips

- It may take a few days for people to respond to any messages you send to a mailing list.
- When you reply to a message, include the point you are responding to in the original message. (This is called quoting.)
- Create a separate folder in your e-mail program to hold your mailing list e-mails.
- Follow the mailing list's guidelines about the kind of messages you can send in.
- Unsubscribe if you are going away, and resubscribe when you return, or you may end up with hundreds of unread e-mails.

16 • Visit a chat room

You don't need to download a special program to use a Web-based chat room. These are Web sites on the Internet where you can chat to other visitors on the site.

You should only use monitored chat rooms. These are sites where the content of chat is monitored to prevent any bad language, bullying, or inappropriate topics of conversation. Using these sites will make your visits safer and more enjoyable. The first time you visit a chat room, find out what people are chatting about before you join in. (This is called lurking.)

The **Headbone Web site** has good, well monitored chat rooms. To enter them, click on *hbzChat* from the drop-down menu on the home page. You'll need to get a login-ID and password before you can enter a room. Once you have logged-in, select a room from the list, and click on *Go chat* to enter it. You can either send messages for everyone in the room to read, or you can send them to one person only.

Emoticons

Emoticons, or smileys, are a great way of expressing yourself when you're e-mailing or chatting online. They're funny little sideways faces, made out of keyboard characters, which help to express your tone in an e-mail. Here are a few to get you started:

:-)	Happy
:-(	Sad
:-D	Laughing
:-0	Suprised
:-P	Sticking tongue out
;-)	Winking
>:-(	Angry

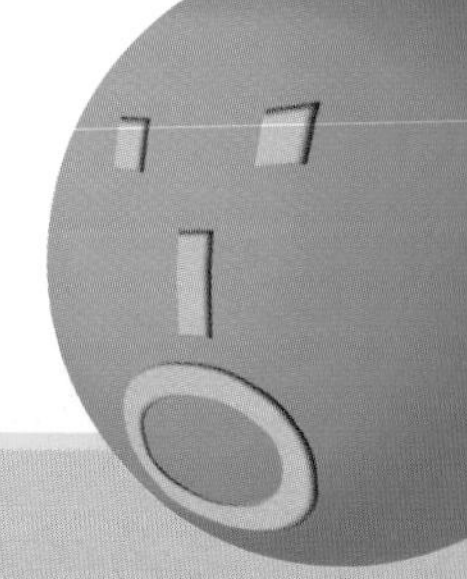

Finding out about films

Movie buffs everywhere love the Internet, because it has a wealth of information about new and current films. You can watch previews for future releases, read reviews on current movies and take a trip behind the scenes.

17 • Find movies in your area

You can use the Internet to plan a trip to see a movie. One site you may find useful is the **Internet Movie Database Web site**. It contains a set of links to sites where you can find movies that are showing in cinemas across the world.

When you visit the site, click on your country from the list which appears to see links to listings for your area. Simply click on the relevant link to find information about current films showing locally.

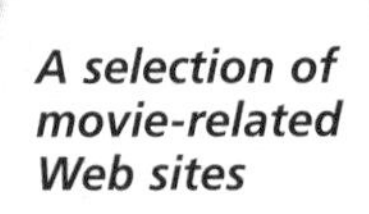

A selection of movie-related Web sites

Courtesy Warner Bros. Online

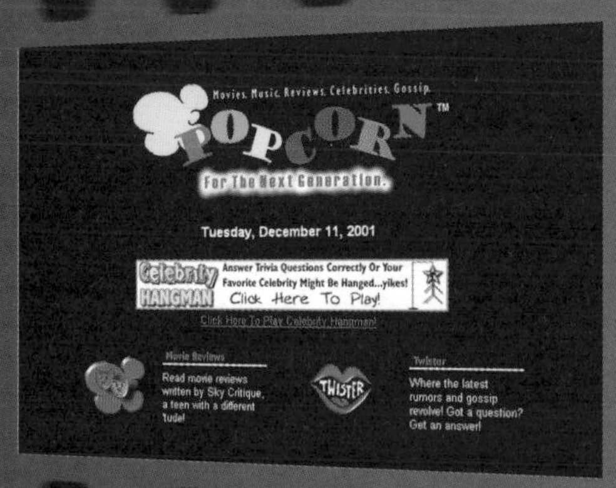

18 • Watch a film preview

The Internet is a great place to find out about up-and-coming movies. There are lots of sites where you can watch previews of future releases, often long before they are shown elsewhere.

Since previews are video clips, you'll need a plug-in to view them (see projects 7 and 8). You can download the *QuickTime* plug-in at the **Apple Web site**, where you'll also find a huge selection of previews to watch.

The trailer will be shown in a box in your browser's window and you'll hear the soundtrack through your speakers or headphones. Click on the buttons at the bottom of the box to rewind or fast-forward the trailer.

Most of the previews on this site also have links to the movie's official Web site, where you can find release dates and more information.

If you downloaded *RealPlayer®* in project 7, you can use it to watch lots of movie trailers. Click on the *RealPlayer* icon on your desktop. You'll see a list of channels on the left of the screen. Select *The Screening Room* channel to see a list of current previews. Then, click on one to download it.

Previews can take a long time to download, so be certain that you want to watch the one you've chosen before you begin to download it.

19 • Go behind the scenes

Have you ever wondered what goes on behind the scenes in movie-making? At the **Annenberg/CPB site** you can visit their online Cinema Exhibition, where you can explore all aspects of film-making, from screenwriting and acting, to directing and editing. There are lots of hands-on activities to take part in.

Try writing your own dialogue for a scene, then find out what the job of producer involves. (Hands-on activities are marked by an old-fashioned "clapper board" on the left of the text. Click on it to access the activity.)

Courtesy Warner Bros. Online

20 • Read a movie review

If you've heard about a film, but aren't really sure whether you want to go and see it, why not read an online review? There are lots of sites on the Internet where you can read reviews for the latest film releases.

The **BBC Films Web site** has a good review section. Click on *Reviews*, from the list on the left of the page to access it. Each entry has a brief synopsis and a star rating between 1-5. If you click on the title of a film, you'll be taken to a page with a full review and lots of background information.

Once you've seen the film, why not add your opinion to the Web site? On the left of the page you'll see a "rate this film" box. Select a star rating between 1-5 (1=bad, 5=excellent) and click on *Submit*. You'll find the average rating at the top of the page.

You can also test your knowledge of the film you've just watched in the quizzes section of the site or read interviews with the stars. To access these sections, click on *Interviews* or *Quizzes* from the list on the left of the page.

Music online

Whether you want to listen to music, read about it, make it or download it, you'll find lots of resources on the Internet.

21 • Read a music e-zine

There are lots of online magazines, or e-zines, on the Internet, covering every topic or hobby you can think of. Some are sister sites which accompany printed magazines, while others are only available online.

There are some particularly good and informative music e-zines, which will keep you up-to-date on everything from album and single releases, to tour dates and chart positions. There are often interviews with bands, music video clips to watch, competitions and music polls to take part in, and you can sometimes buy albums online.

The **Popworld site** is a glitzy, funky e-zine which concentrates on the world of pop music. The **NME site** is the sister site of the printed music magazine and has more indepth content on a broader music scene. The **dotmusic Web site** is an online music store, but it has lots of music news coverage and is often considered as an e-zine. You could do a keyword search to find a music magazine which suits your musical tastes. Use your favourite genre of music as a keyword and add **+e-zine** or **+"online magazine"**.

22 • Download a mobile ring tone

You can personalize your mobile phone by downloading musical ring tones from the Web. There is a wide selection of tunes available, including the latest chart hits and TV show theme tunes, or you can compose your own.

Most sites charge a small amount for each download (see projects 43 and 47 for help on paying). Some ring tones only work with a particular brand of phone (such as Nokia), so make sure yours is compatible. You'll also need to provide your mobile telephone number, so that the site can send the ring tone directly to your phone. Try visiting the **Ringtones.com Web site**.

A selection of music e-zines

23 • Mix your own beats

Have you ever fancied yourself as a club DJ? At the **Turntables Web site**, you can test your skills, using their DJ Simulator. You'll need the *Macromedia® Flash™* plug-in, which you can download via a link on the site (if you haven't already done so). Click on the *new school version* to enter. A new window will open containing the interactive *Flash™* animation.

***Find out what it is like to mix and scratch records using the DJ Simulator at the* Turntables Web site.**

Use your mouse to explore the screen. You'll find that you can select records and play them on the turntables, adjust the lighting, get the crowd cheering and have your own personal MC shouting out to them. Be sure to have a go at record scratching while you're there.

24 • Download MP3 music files

It is possible to download music from the Internet and store it on your computer's hard drive, but it can take up a lot of memory space. MP3 files are currently the best and most popular way of storing music. These are heavily compressed files, so they take up much less space. The sound quality is not damaged during the compression: they are usually about as clear as a CD.

You can play them on your computer and listen to them through your speakers, or you can buy a portable MP3 player. This looks like a personal stereo, and you can use it to listen to music anywhere, but it works in a different way. Portable MP3 players have an inbuilt sound card, which you copy MP3 files onto.

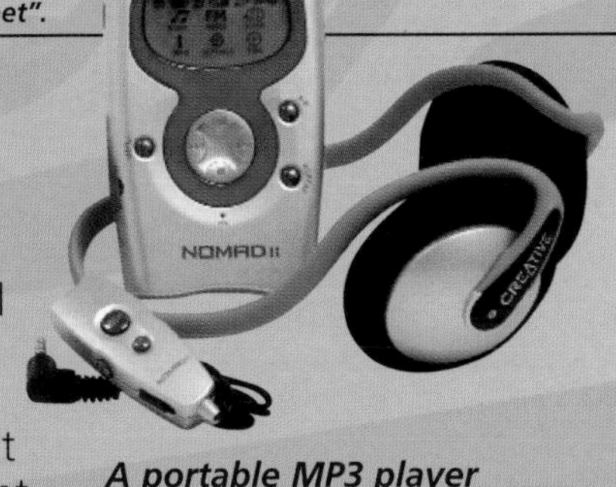

A portable MP3 player

In order to play MP3 files on your computer, you need a media player, such as *RealJukebox® Basic,* which you can download at the **Real.com Web site**. If you downloaded *RealPlayer®* in project 7, you may have already downloaded *RealJukebox Basic*. If not, scroll down the home page, and click on the link to download the free version. You could also download the *Surreal.FX Basic* program. This is a *RealJukebox Basic* accessory which plays animations that dance to the beat of your MP3 files. From the home page, click on *Accessories,* then *RealJukebox Accessories,* to download it.

The **MP3.com Web site** has a huge range of MP3 files to download. You can browse them by style, such as *Latin* or *Jazz.* Generally, you will have to pay to download MP3 files, but some sites offer promotional tracks, which are free to copy, especially by new bands.

The* Surreal.FX *screen

Copyright caution

You should be cautious when it comes to downloading tracks from the Internet. Remember that, like pictures and books, music is subject to copyright. Only copy tracks from official sites; otherwise you could be breaking the law. Always make sure the site clearly states that you have permission to download each track.

The world of sport

The Internet is a rich source of information for fans of all kinds of sports. As well as following the team you support's progress, you can use the Internet to get the latest scores, learn a new sport, join a fantasy league, or investigate future sporting events.

***You can find out about your Olympic wrestling team via the* Olympics' Web site.**

25 • Join a fantasy league

If you've always fancied your chances as a sports manager or coach, you can put yourself to the test by taking part in an online fantasy league.

Fantasy sports are competitions where you can draft your own dream team of professional players and compete against other people's teams around the world. In most cases, you are given a pretend budget to spend on players. Once you have submitted your team, its success depends on how your players perform in their real-life games.

Soccer fans can try managing a team at the **Telegraph Premier League Web site**, while basketball, baseball, ice hockey, motor racing and inline skating fans can all visit the **Sports Illustrated Kids Web site** to compete in a fantasy league.

As each sport is different, you will need to read the individual guides on how to play and how to get started. At Sports Illustrated Kids, you can access a guide by selecting a sport and then clicking on *The rules*. At the Telegraph Premier League site, click on *Tell me more*.

26 • Preview a future event

Most major international sporting events set up an official Web site before the event, where you can find out about everything from ticket sales and event timetables, to maps and hotel accommodation.

For example, you can find out about the next Summer and Winter Olympics by visiting the **official Olympics Web site.** There you'll currently find links to the Salt Lake City 2002 site, the Athens 2004 site and even the Torino 2006 site.

You can also link to your country's site to find out how the national team is preparing for the next event. Click on *National Olympic Committees,* and browse for your team.

The* Olympics *home page has links to official event and national team sites, and you can also visit the online Olympic Museum.

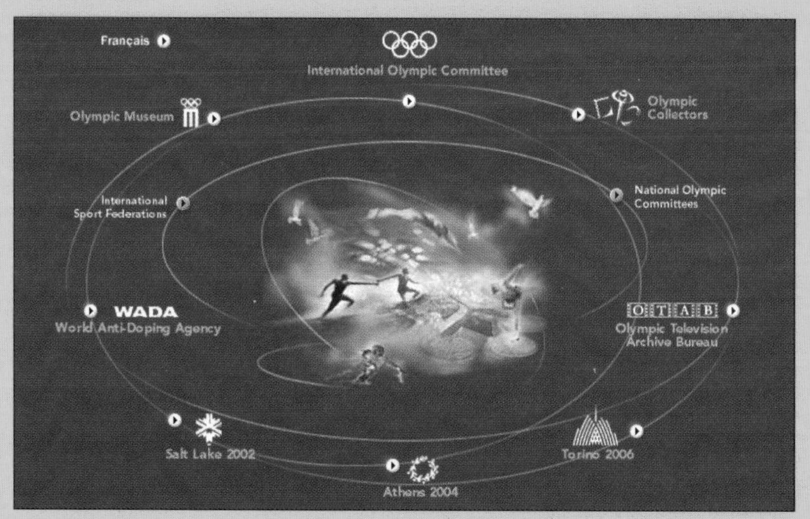

27 • Follow your team

Whatever sport you're into, most major league teams have an official Web site, so you can follow their progress and support them throughout the season.

As well as fixtures, scores and team news, lots of official sites have extra features and activities. These include: virtual stadium tours, mailing lists (see project 11), and desktop themes to download, such as wallpapers (see project 80) and screen savers (see project 67). There are often player halls of fame, and you can sometimes listen to match commentaries.

To find your team's official site, try doing a keyword search using the team's name, the category of sport and adding **+official**.

At the* FC Barcelona Web site*, you can take a virtual tour of the stadium, get the latest team news, and shop for club memorabilia.

28 • Learn a new sport

Lots of people use the Internet to find out about a sport they follow, but why not use it to improve your own sporting talents? At the **SportsID Web site**, there are over 1,500 short video clips for you to watch. They feature professional sport stars demonstrating their tips and techniques.

On the home page, click on a sport from the list on the left, and select a skill from the list that appears. To play the video, you need a plug-in, such as *RealPlayer®* or *QuickTime*. Use projects 7 and 8 to help you install one. Then, when you come to play the clip, select your plug-in from the list on the right of the video screen.

The* SportsID *video screen

29 • Get the latest score

News agencies and broadcasting companies often maintain Web pages which are constantly updated with sporting information and results from around the world. One very thorough online sports service is the **CNN/Sports Illustrated site**, which covers everything from tennis to snowboarding.

If you are visiting this site to get the latest scores while a game is in progress, you need to click on your browser's *Refresh* or *Reload* button from time to time, to ensure that the information on the page you are looking at is completely up-to-date. This will instruct your browser to download the latest version of the Web page, which should contain the current scores.

Playing games online

A scene from **AquaNox**, *a science fiction, action game*

The Internet is a popular place to play games. Whether you're into action, adventure, strategy, classic, racing, puzzle, card or simulation games, you'll find them all widely available to download, or to play online with other players around the world.

30 • Play a game online

A good place to start, if you're new to the world of computer games, is the **Kids Domain Online Games site**. This site has a mixture of games which cater for lots of different age groups, and they are all completely free to play.

You need various plug-ins (see project 7), such as *Macromedia® Shockwave®,* to play most of the games on this site. You may already have downloaded some of them for other projects in this book. If not, there are links to sites where you can download the right one.

When you visit the site, you'll see a page of categories, such as "sports" or "brain games". If there is a huge list of games in that category, they will be organized according to which plug-in they require, as well as by age group. (Games for younger players are listed first.)

Some of the games listed on this site are part of Kids Domain, while others are on different game sites. You'll jump to the start of a game on another site when you click on its link. Once you have finished playing the game, hit your *Back* button to return to Kids Domain.

31 • Join a game of chess online

If you prefer traditional board games to the usual computer games, visit the **Yahooligans! Games Web site**. At this site, you can play computerized versions of traditional games, such as chess, checkers and backgammon, online against other Yahooligans! players anywhere in the world.

This works like a chat room (see project 16), but instead of joining in a conversation, you can join a game in progress, start your own, or watch other people's. You need to make sure you're computer is Java-enabled. To do this, click on your browser's *Tools* menu, select *Internet Options...*, and tick the "Java-enabled" box. For each game, you'll need to download a Java™ applet (a small program) before you can start playing. You'll be taken directly to the download when you access the game for the first time. You'll find a list of instructions for each game by clicking on *Yahooligans! Games Rules*, on the home page.

Here are some of the games you will find on the Internet.

Virtual Pool 2

Amped: Freestyle Snowboarding

Toon Car

32 • Compete in a multi-user game

If you're a serious game player, you can play "multi-user games". These are action, strategy and role-playing games (RPG) which you can play online against people anywhere in the world. To play a multi-user game online, you'll need a copy of the game and an Internet connection.

Information about the game is stored in two places. Parts of it, especially the game's graphics, are stored on your computer (known as the client computer). This prevents you from having to download the graphics every time you play the game. The rest of the information, including details about each player, is stored on the site which hosts the game. The players connect to the host site when they want to play against others. The games use a special "client program" to transfer information between the client computers and the host site. The **Games Domain site** has reviews of the latest game releases and there are demonstration versions (demos) to download for free. (Usually you can play the demo by yourself, but you have to buy the full version before you can compete online.)

System requirements

• Always read the instructions and "system requirements" section carefully *before* you download a game, to make sure your computer is compatible. To play some multi-user games, you'll need a very fast Internet connection and a more powerful computer than the one outlined on page 6.
• You may need to buy some extra hardware, such as a graphics card, before you can play some games. (You'll need at least a 32 bit card with 2MB of Video RAM.)

This is a scene from* EverQuest*, a role-playing game set in a fantasy world. You can play with over 1,000 players at any one time.

33 • Race cars online

Computer game graphics are constantly improving. There are lots of games available on the Internet which have amazing 3-D graphics. You can race cars and almost feel as though you are behind the wheel.

Most games have an official Web site, providing information about the game, screen shots, demos and details of where you can buy it. (The **Games Domain site** has links to lots of official sites.) *NASCAR® Racing 4* is an impressive 3-D racing game, by Sierra™. You can download a demo version and find out more at the **Sierra™ Web site**. (Use projects 7-9 to help you.)

***Scenes from* NASCAR® Racing 4**

Digital photography

If you're into photography, you can get creative with your pictures and share them with others using a variety of Internet resources. These projects will introduce you to creating digital pictures and will show you how to have some fun with them.

You might like to use some of the pictures you create to decorate your own Web page. (Pages 56-59 explore Web page design.)

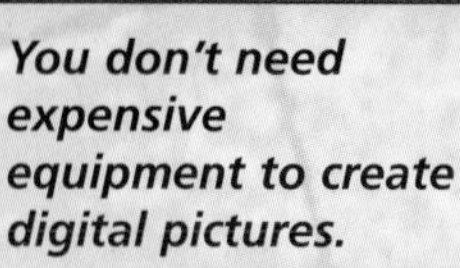

You don't need expensive equipment to create digital pictures.

34 • Make a digital picture

Before you can create special effects with your pictures, send them by e-mail, or print them from your computer, you need to convert them to computer files, so that your computer can understand and process them. Pictures stored as computer files are called digital pictures.

There are several ways to make digital pictures. You can use a digital camera, or a scanner ~ or, when you take a roll of film to be developed, you can ask the developers to put the pictures onto a picture CD which you will be able to open on your computer.

Digital cameras look quite similar to ordinary cameras, but instead of storing the images on film, they are stored on the camera as computer data. You can copy digital picture files from the camera to your computer when you connect them to each other.

Digital cameras are quick and easy to use, but if you don't have one, you can use a scanner to covert your ordinary photographic prints into digital files. Page 7 and project 79 explain how this works. Save all your digital pictures in your *Projects* folder (see page 7), so that they are easy to find later. If you just want to have some fun with your pictures, you can scan them at a low-resolution of about 75 dpi.

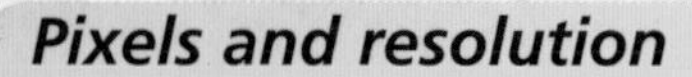

Pixels and resolution

- The pictures you see on your computer screen consist of millions of tiny dots, called pixels. Your computer stores information about the position and colour of every pixel in a picture.
- The number of pixels a picture contains is known as its "resolution". Resolution is measured in dots per inch (dpi).
- Pictures which contain lots of pixels are "high-resolution" images, and pictures which contain a small number of pixels are called "low-resolution" images.
- High-resolution images are much clearer, than low-resolution images. But, because they contain more pixels, they are large files and take a long time to download.

You don't notice that digital pictures are made up of dots until you see them close-up.

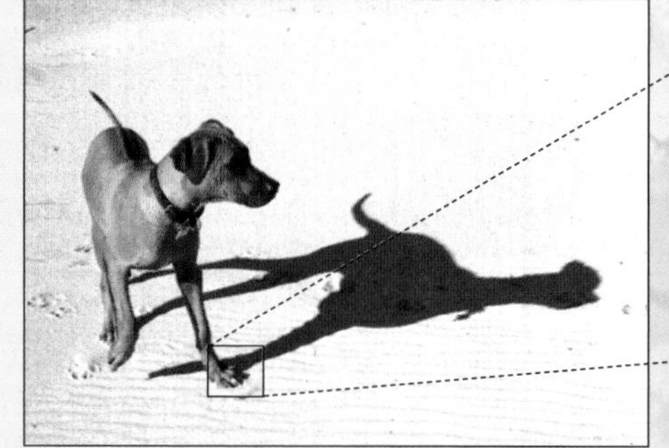

Here, you can see the pixels clearly.

35 • Create special effects

Once you have saved your digital pictures onto your computer (see project 34), you can visit the **Kodak PictureCenter Web site**. At this site, you can improve the quality of your pictures, or have some fun with them by adding crazy effects. To do this, you need to register with the site, then copy the pictures from your computer to the Kodak PictureCenter Web site. This is called uploading.

To register, click on *Join Kodak.com*, under the *Manage* menu, and fill in the online form. (You'll need to login everytime you visit the site.) Once you have registered, click on *Manage*, and select *Upload Pictures from Your Computer.* On the screen that appears, click on *Browse...*

***You can transform your pictures with crazy effects at the* Kodak PictureCenter Web site.**

Find your *Projects* folder (where you saved your pictures in project 34) and select a picture to upload. Double click on it, and the filename will be copied onto the upload screen. Click on *Upload now!,* and your picture should appear on the Kodak PictureCenter screen. It will remain on the site until you delete it.

You can improve the quality of your pictures using the tools in the *Edit* menu. To create some crazy effects, click on an effect from the *Play* menu, such as *Cartoon Maker*. Some of the effects you can create are shown above. When you have finished and saved your picture, you can copy it back onto your computer and print it. Click on the *Manage* menu, then on *Download Your Pictures to Your Computer.* Follow the on-screen instructions.

You can use your uploaded pictures to create e-cards to send to friends.

36 • Share pictures with friends

The Internet has made it easy to share pictures with friends and family. You can send digital pictures as an e-mail attachment. Project 50 explains how to do this.

Alternatively, you could use one of the pictures you transformed in project 35 to create an e-card (see project 12) at the **Kodak PictureCenter Web site**. You can even add your own captions to the picture. To make an e-card, select a picture you've saved on the site, then click on the *Share* menu. From the list of options, select *Talk it up!*. Now choose a speech balloon style, type in your caption, and click on *Continue*. You can click and drag the balloon to position it. Finally, click on *Done*.

You need to add a personal message before you send the e-card. Then, type the e-mail address of the person you're sending it to and your own e-mail address (so they know who to reply to). Finally, click on *Send it!*.

Printing your pictures

High-resolution pictures use a lot of ink when you print them, and the ink often smudges. There are two things you can do to reduce this problem. You should use a good quality paper for printing pictures. You can buy special photo-quality paper from a computer or stationery store. Alternatively, you can set your printer to the "economy" or "draft" setting. This means that it will use less ink, and will be less likely to smudge. (You should find this setting under *Properties...* in your printer menu.)

Food and recipes

If you're in the mood for cooking, you'll find millions of mouth-watering recipes for dishes from all over the world on the Internet. There is lots of information about healthy eating and you can sometimes order meals online.

***You'll find hundreds of cookie recipes at the* Cookie Tin Web site.**

37 • Find a recipe online

You can find the recipe for a specific dish by searching the Internet using the names of its main ingredients. This is also a good way to find out what you could make with any ingredients you already have at home. For example, a search using the keywords **+recipe +chicken +mushrooms** would give you a list of recipes which might include chicken and mushroom pie, and chicken casserole.

The **BBC Food Web site** has an excellent recipe section with lots of mouth-watering ideas. You can browse through a huge range of recipes supplied by top celebrity chefs, including Jamie Oliver and Gary Rhodes. If you're looking for something in particular, you could try using the recipe finder search engine. To reach the recipe section of the site, click on *Recipes*, from the list on the left of the BBC Food home page.

If you need a little help in the kitchen, you can post questions for top chefs to answer in the *Ask the Chef* section of the site. There is also a useful glossary of cooking terms, where you can find out about lots of weird and wonderful ingredients.

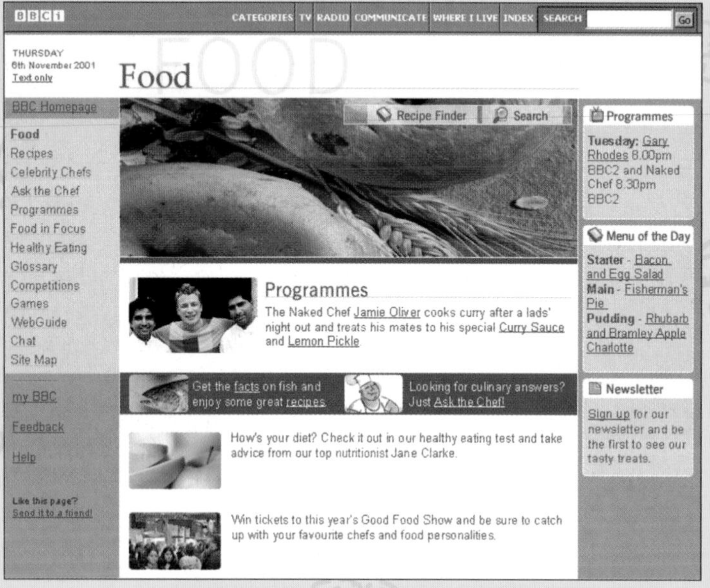

The* BBC Food Web site *is full of recipes ideas.

38 • Order food online

To order a meal online, you have to find a local restaurant which offers an online order service. You place your order by filling in an online form. Then the food is delivered directly to your home when it is ready. (You will either have to pay for the food online, or when it is delivered.)

You could do a keyword search to find sites which offer this service. Enter as keywords the type of food you want, the word online, and the name of your town, or city. For example, a search using **+pizza +online +"London"** will produce a list of pizza restaurants in London that take online orders.

In the U.K.,* Leaping Salmon *deliver meals to your door in a kit-form.

39 • Analyse your diet

We all have good intentions when it comes to healthy eating, but sometimes it is difficult to know which foods are good for you and which are not. The Internet is a brilliant source of information on healthy eating.

At the **BBC Healthy Eating Web site**, you can do a nutrition quiz to analyse what you eat. Enter how many portions of each major food group (such as fruit and vegetables, or meats and fish) you eat on a daily basis and make sure you don't leave out any sneaky snacks. Once you have clicked on *submit*, you will be given a breakdown of your eating habits, and advice on what you need to eat more, or less, of for a balanced and healthy diet.

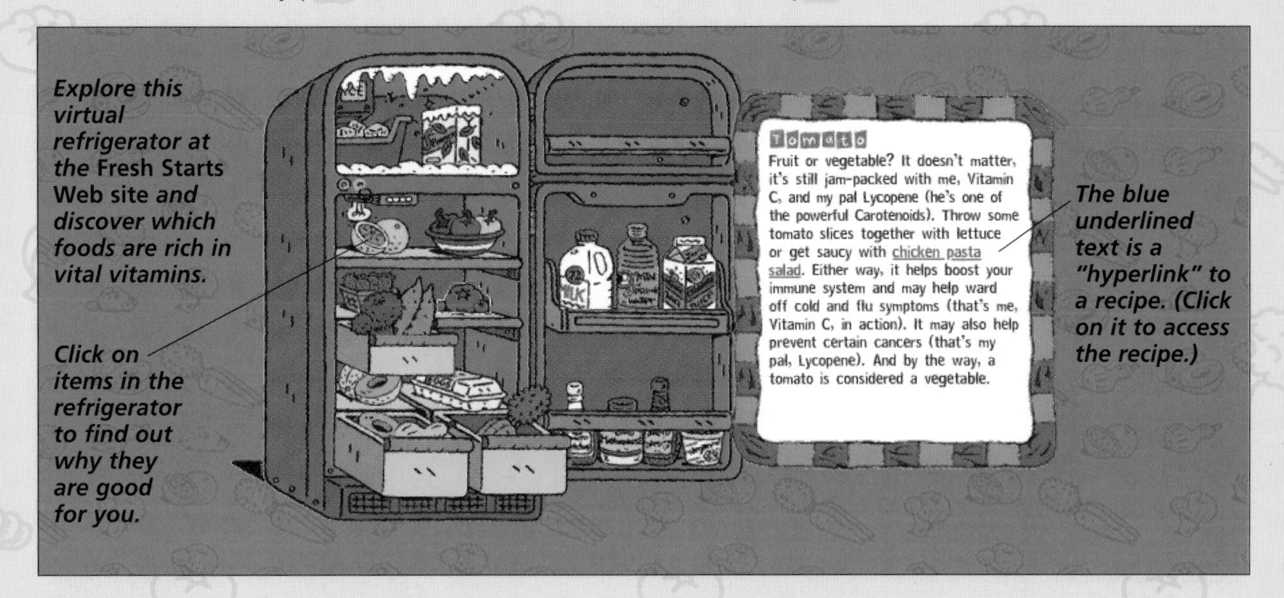

Explore this virtual refrigerator at the Fresh Starts Web site and discover which foods are rich in vital vitamins.

Click on items in the refrigerator to find out why they are good for you.

The blue underlined text is a "hyperlink" to a recipe. (Click on it to access the recipe.)

40 • Explore a food timeline

At the **Food Timeline Web site** you can follow the development of food and recipes from as early as 17,000BC through to the present day. Did you know, for example, that chewing gum can be traced back as far as 4,500BC? Or that hamburgers, often thought of as a great American speciality, reportedly date back to 13th century Germany?

On the left of the timeline there are links to pages of interest about each food item, and on the right are links to recipes which have been adapted for modern cooking methods.

If you are also interested in food culture, click on *Culinary History Timeline* at the top of the page and follow the additional links there.

41 • Publish your recipe online

Some Web sites encourage you to contribute your own recipes, which are then put on their site. The **Recipe Book Online Recipe Archive Web site** has a large collection.

To add your own to the site, click on *Submit recipe.* Fill in the online form, including the title of your recipe, the ingredients, and the preparation instructions, and click on *Submit recipe* at the bottom of the form.

Your recipe will be added to the Web site. You can see it by returning to the home page. Then, click on the category you placed the recipe in (e.g. *meats*, *soups* or *desserts*) and look for the title of your recipe in the list.

If you put a recipe on a site, make sure that it's worded carefully and clearly, so that people can follow it easily.

Books and writing online

When the Internet was first developed, lots of people were worried that it might mean the end of traditional paper books. Instead, it has just made buying them easier. Many sites do offer electronic books, or e-books (versions which you download directly from the Internet, rather than buying them in paper form), but paper books are still much more popular.

You can read animated poems on the* BBC Web site's *poetry page.

42 • Watch a book animation

You can watch a brilliant animated history of books at the **BBC Web site**. It begins back in 50,000 BC, with early cave paintings, and tracks the development of books through every age in history, right up to the present day. It's full of fascinating trivia. Did you know, for example, that Daniel Defoe was only paid £10 for writing *Robinson Crusoe*. To see the animation, you'll need the *Macromedia® Flash™* plug-in (see projects 7 and 8). Switch on your speakers, and click on *hi-tech,* for the really flashy version.

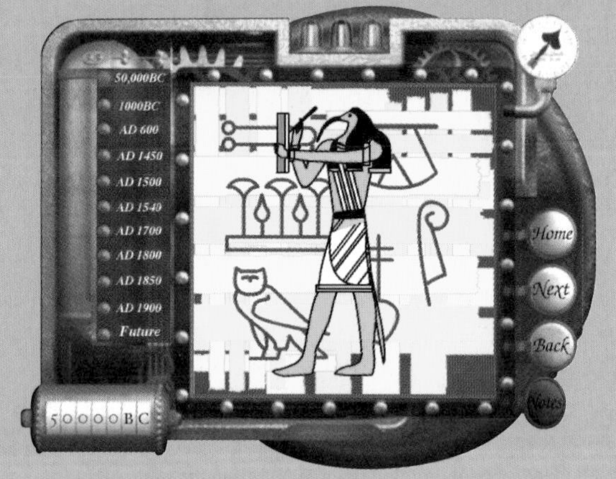

A still from the* BBC site's *animated history of books

43 • Shop at an Internet bookstore

You can buy paper books online from Internet bookstores. One big advantage is that they offer millions of titles, far more than you'll find in any store. They also feature articles about new books and authors, comments from readers, and recommendations.

One of the most popular Internet bookstores is **Amazon**. To look at the books available to buy, click on *Books* from the list of categories on the home page. You can use the search engine to find a book, or you can click on a category, such as *Fiction*, to browse. If you find a book you'd like to buy, you need to add it to your shopping basket. (This is sometimes called a shopping cart or trolley). These are used on many online shopping sites to collect all the items you are going to buy. To add an item, select it and click on *Add to Shopping Basket*.

To pay for your books, you have to complete an online form. You'll need to provide a delivery address and state how you are going to pay for them. (You'll also have to pay a delivery charge.) Most people who buy things online pay for their goods with a credit card. (To buy things online you usually have to be over 18. If you're not, ask someone who is to help you.) Pages 32-33 explain how to pay for things online.

amazon.com

Amazon *and* Fnac *both have lots of international Web sites where you can buy books online.*

44 • Find a book online

Many famous works of literature are published on the Internet. You can access over 5,000 electronic versions of books at the **Internet Public Library Web site**.

To help you find a particular play, poem or novel, this site includes a search engine. If, for example, you want to find one of Shakespeare's sonnets, click on *Online Texts* on the Internet Public Library home page. Then, you'll see a search page. Type "**Shakespeare Sonnets**" into the box, and click on *Search*. A list of links to online versions of a book called *The Sonnets* should appear.

Click on one of these links to download the book. This may take a few minutes. Scroll down the page to find the sonnet you want to read. You could also print the page by clicking on *Print* in the *File* menu.

The* Achuka Web site *is a portal. It has links to a whole world of children's books and related Web sites. You can access publishers', authors' and Illustrators' sites, as well as Internet bookstores.

45 • Add to a neverending story

Some of the stories you'll find on the Internet have been written jointly by a large number of people. They are called neverending stories. A neverending story starts when someone publishes the beginning of a story on a Web site and invites other people to send in contributions to continue the plot. These sections are put straight onto the site, so that Internet users can follow the story as it develops.

The* Writers' Window *site

A good place to read and join a neverending story is the **English Online ~ Writers' Window site**. There are a selection of stories for you to add to each week, with titles such as "*The Mysterious Light*". Once you have read the story so far, fill in the online form at the bottom of the page, adding your contribution. Anything you submit will appear on the site immediately.

Budding writers can also publish their own poems and stories on this site for other visitors to read. To add your work, click on the *Write a story* or *Write a poem* link on the home page.

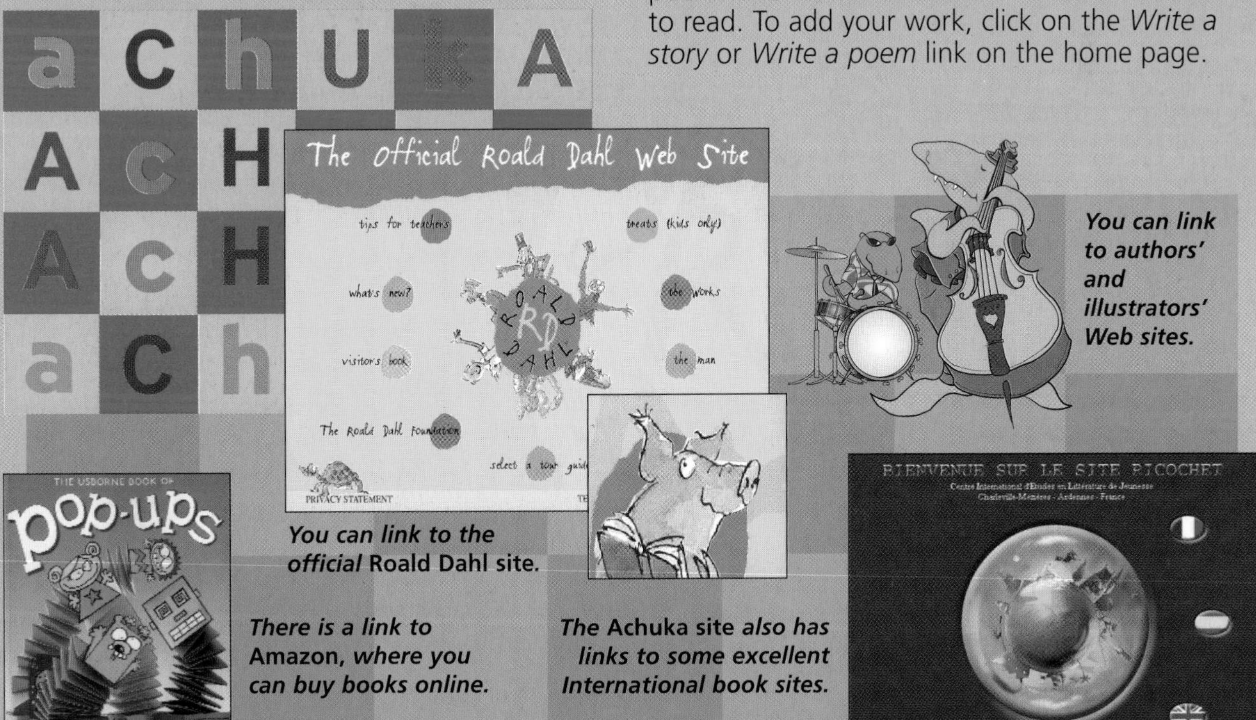

You can link to authors' and illustrators' Web sites.

You can link to the official* Roald Dahl *site.

There is a link to Amazon, where you can buy books online.

The* Achuka *site also has links to some excellent International book sites.

Shopping online

More and more people are turning to the Internet to do their shopping. There are now many stores which only operate on the Internet and don't run any high street branches.

You can buy almost anything online, from clothes, gifts and CDs, to your weekly grocery shop. Lots of collectors use it to track down rare items and memorabilia.

You can order flowers online to be delivered anywhere in the world.

You can shop online for delicious chocolates, or send them as a gift to someone.

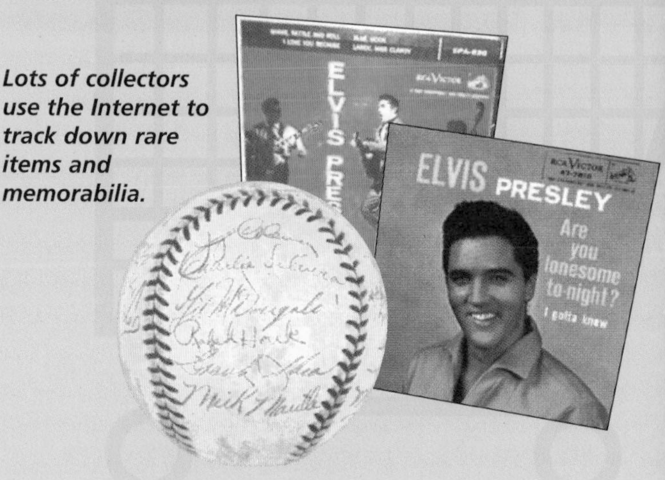

Lots of collectors use the Internet to track down rare items and memorabilia.

46 • Visit a shopping mall

An online shopping mall (or directory) is a portal Web site (see project 5) which brings together lots of shopping sites. You can visit many stores on one site, just as you would do at a real shopping mall.

The **Ask Web site** has a useful shopping directory with links to some of the best online shopping sites. You can use the search engine to find what you are looking for, or you can browse the shops by clicking on a category, such as *Music CDs* or *Gifts*.

At some online shopping malls, including the Ask site and the **ShopSmart site**, you can compare prices across all stores in the directory. So you can make sure you're getting the best deal on the market. Projects 43 and 47 explain how to pay for things online. If you're under 18, you may need to ask an adult for help.

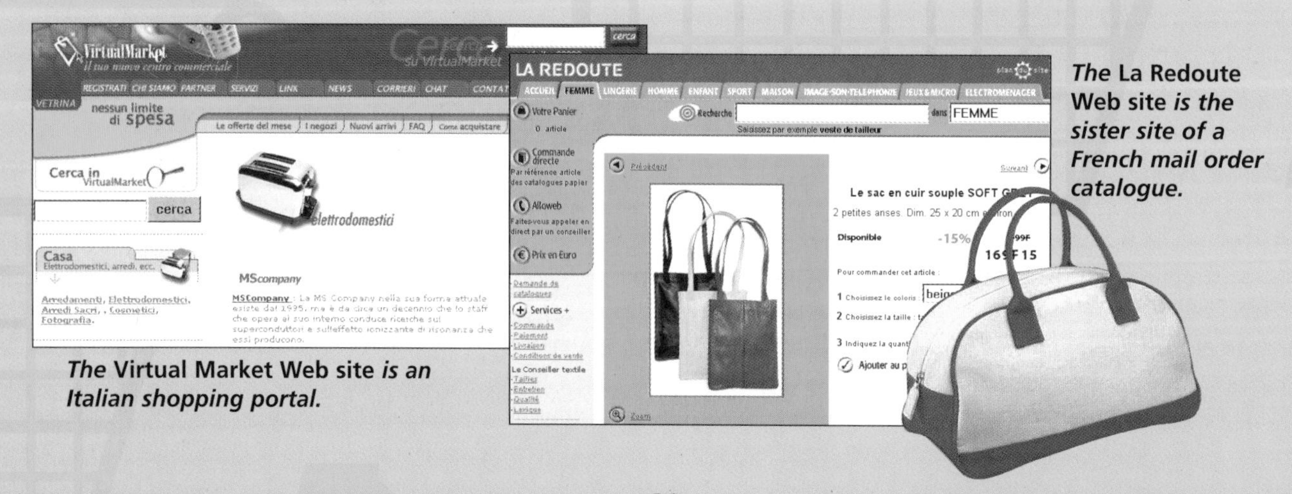

The Virtual Market Web site ***is an Italian shopping portal.***

The La Redoute Web site ***is the sister site of a French mail order catalogue.***

47 • Use electronic cash

Some people pay for things online using electronic cash, or eCash®. To use eCash, you set up a special eCash account through your bank, and then transfer money into it from your ordinary bank account. The money can be used to buy goods at online stores, instead of paying by credit card. Unlike a credit card, you don't have to be 18 to use it.

If you're interested in using eCash, search for your own bank's Web site and find out whether it offers an eCash service. If it does, it should also have full instructions on how to set up an account. The **Digicash® Web site** has more information and a useful demo. (You'll need the *Macromedia® Flash*™ plug-in ~ see projects 7 and 8 for help.)

The Digicash® demo explains how eCash® works in six stages.

Security

When you pay for things online, make sure the site uses a "secure" server. This means that personal information sent to the site, including addresses and credit card details, can't be seen by anyone else. The information is encrypted (turned into a code), when it is sent across the Internet, and changed back when it is received.

A window will appear to tell you when you are entering, and leaving, a secure Web page. You should also look for a locked padlock symbol which will be displayed in the bottom left corner of your browser window.

Shopping tips

- Try to buy items from Internet companies that are based in your country, otherwise you may have to pay tax on the goods.
- Make sure that the delivery charge isn't too high and that the items can be delivered to your country. This isn't always possible.
- Be sure the item you buy is exactly what you want, and that you can return it if you change your mind.
- Only shop with companies that have stores on the high street, or with well-known Internet companies.
- Some companies like to send e-mails to customers, about special offers and sales. If you don't want to receive these, tick the box which says so on your order form.

48 • Go bargain hunting

It costs a lot less to run a Web site than a whole chain of stores around the country, so you can often get much better deals by shopping online. One popular online discount store is the **Haburi Web site**. This site sells designer clothes and accessories at a much cheaper rate than usual store prices. Items cost between 25-75% less than on the high street.

At the Haburi Web site you can get high fashion clothes and accessories at a much lower price than on the high street.

If you're an animal lover, you can use the Internet to get advice on looking after your pet, explore wildlife scenes, find amazing wildlife photos and listen to the call of wild animals and birds.

49 • Get help with your pet

No matter how unusual your pet is, you'll find lots of helpful advice on the Internet, on everything from diet and exercise, to health and training problems.

The **BBC Web site** has a good page on looking after pets. There are several question and answer sections, providing advice from vets and animal experts. You'll find answers to questions such as: "How can I stop my cat from digging up next door's flowerbeds?", or "Why has my rabbit started gnawing at his food bowl?" If you're thinking about getting a new pet, there are also some useful fact files, which may help you choose the right one.

***You can find out how to keep your dog, and other pets, healthy and happy at the* BBC Web site.**

50 • Send a wildlife picture by e-mail

Publishing companies use the Internet to search for photos to include in books and magazines, and photographers often display their work on personal Web sites. So, there is lots of amazing wildlife photography to see online. If you find a picture that you'd like to share with a friend, you can send it to them as an attachment in an e-mail.

One place where you can see amazing photographs is at the **Nature Photo Index site**. This site has links to nature photo galleries and libraries which have sites on the Internet. You can browse for pictures by clicking on *Galleries,* or you can use their search engine. (Select *Galleries* from the drop-down menu and type a keyword.)

When you have found a picture to send, click on it with your right mouse button. Select *Save Picture As* (or something similar) from the menu which appears. In the next dialog box, select the *Projects* folder you created on page 7 from the *Save in* box. The picture will already have a filename, so you can simply click on *OK* to save it.

To attach the picture to an e-mail in *Microsoft® Outlook® Express*, (see pages 14-15), begin by composing your message. Then, click on *Insert*, followed by *File Attachment...* In the next window, browse for your *Projects* folder in the *Look in* box. When you've found it, select a picture, and click on *Attach*. When you are ready, connect to the Internet, and send the message in the usual way.

At the* Nature Photo Index site *you'll find pictures of wild cats like this one.

51 • Watch animals in the wild

Web cameras, or Webcams, transmit live pictures over the Internet and are a great way to watch animals in the wild. The **Africam site** has Webcams set up around a large game reserve at Kruger National Park in South Africa. You can see if any animals are grazing at one of the waterholes, for example, or take a look at the Seabed cam for a fishy encounter.

Select a Webcam from the home page and it will appear in a new window. Unfortunately, there won't always be animals in view on the Webcams, so you may have to check back again frequently. This site takes a long time to download, but be patient, as it's well worth it.

You might meet some zebras at the **Africam site.**

52 • Explore an underwater scene

At the **National Geographic site**, you can use the *Macromedia® Flash™* plug-in to explore an underwater scene, which is based on a National Marine Sanctuary in California, called Monterey Bay. You will dive in a submersible (a small submarine) to the bottom of the bay, encountering the bay's wildlife along the way.

As well as taking the virtual dive, you can read lots of fishy fact files.

You'll need to download the *Flash™* plug-in before you can take the dive. Use the provided link and projects 7 and 8 for extra help. To access the scene, click on *board a submersible* at the bottom of the page, followed by *full version* on the next page. Your journey will start at surface level. Click on any creatures you encounter to learn a little about them (use your mouse to scroll down the text) and click on the diver symbol, on the right, to go deeper.

53 • Listen to birdsongs

One of the great things about the Internet is that it provides access to a whole range of multimedia activities. At the **Enature Web site**, you can listen to over 550 North American birdsongs, using the *RealPlayer®* or *QuickTime* plug-in. (If you haven't already downloaded either of these, use projects 7 and 8 to help you.)

There are lots of sites containing animal sound libraries where you can listen to the calls of wild animals and birds, but the Enature site is particularly good because each birdsong has an accompanying fact file with lots of detailed information. Birds are often shy of humans, so these libraries provide a rare opportunity to listen to some beautiful birdsongs. To hear a birdsong and read the fact file, click on *Bird Audio*, under "Site links" on the home page.

Select a category of bird, such as "owls", and a list will be displayed. Click on *more...*, next to the name of a species, and you will be taken to a page where you can read the fact file and listen to the birdsong.

***A fact file on the Black-necked Stilt from* Enature**

The Internet brings together people from all over the world. This makes it the ideal place to learn about world environmental issues and to discover what you can do to help.

54 • Get a Panda Passport

The **World Wildlife Fund (WWF) Panda Passport Web site** is a new way to campaign for environmental issues over the Internet. Passport holders can take action by signing online petitions, sending e-mails to official figures, making online donations and raising awareness by sending e-postcards to friends.

As a passport holder, you will also receive e-mail newsletters, keeping you up-to-date on campaign progress. There are already many Panda Passport success stories: the Gudar Forest in Spain has been made a legally protected area and a dam was prevented from being built in the Tong River, South Korea.

For every e-mail you send and every other form of action you take, you will receive a virtual stamp in your passport. Each stamp has a points value and as you collect points you will be promoted from a *Level 1 Campaigner* to a *Level 2 Campaigner* and so on.

You need to sign up for a passport before you can take part in the online campaigning. Click on *Join here* on the home page, fill in the online form and click *Register.* To find a campaign, use the clickable map on the home page. Click on an area of the world to zoom in on, then select a campaign from that region.

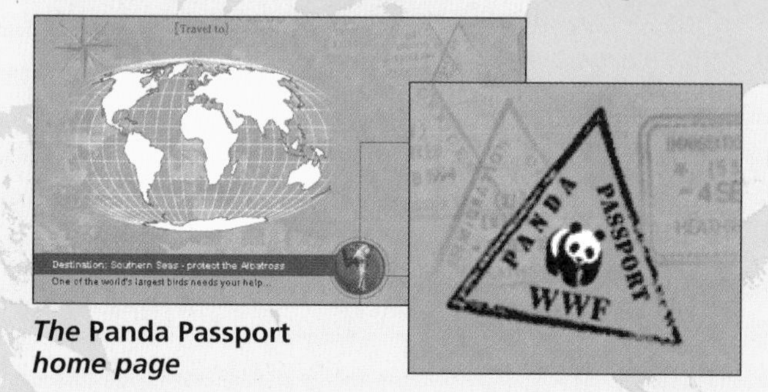

The* Panda Passport *home page

55 • Explore a virtual house

At the **WWF Virtual House Web site**, you can learn how everyday items and activities in the home can profoundly affect the environment. On the home page, read the instructions carefully, then select an area of interest, such as global warming, and click on *Enter house.*

You will now be given a cryptic question and your task is to find an object in the house which answers that question. Click on a room to begin, and then click on any of the items in the room to find out if they answer your question. If a selected item is incorrect, you'll receive some useful ecological information about it instead. To move to another room, click on either of the doorways in the room, or on *Jump to another room.*

***The* WWF Virtual House Web site**

56 • *Explore a world green group*

Groups all over the world have Web sites devoted to the environment. Some international organizations and companies maintain central sites which link to local sites in different countries. One example is the **Greenpeace site**.

Use the central Greenpeace site to find one of the national branches of the organization. On the home page, click on the drop-down menu titled *Greenpeace Worldwide*. You'll see a list of countries. Choose a country and click on it to visit the local Greenpeace site. On some countries' sites you can join Greenpeace online.

The **Greenpeace International Web site**

Use this drop-down menu to link to different branches around the world.

The **Greenpeace Belgium Web site**

A page from the* Greenpeace Belgium Web site *on Nuclear testing

57 • *Visit an endangered species exhibition*

Lots of museums publish detailed Web pages to coincide with their special exhibitions. You can often see museum exhibits online and read more about them. Project 77 shows you where you can find some interesting museum Web sites to visit.

At the **American Museum of Natural History Web site**, you can view an online exhibition about endangered species from around the world.

Click on *Tour the exhibition* on the right of the home page. You will be shown a map of the actual exhibition layout at the museum. You can click on any section to see an exhibit and to find out more about it. Use your browser's *Back* button to return to the clickable map after looking at each exhibit.

Alternatively, you can tour the exhibition by clicking on each of the numbered exhibits in the frame on the left of the screen. Make sure you don't miss the 'VW Bug with Zebra Mussels' exhibit. Click on *The VW Beetle Experiment* to find out what happened to a car that was left at the bottom of a lake for 118 days.

The Internet provides a big helping hand when it comes to homework. As well as being an instant source of a lot of information, it can also make learning much more interactive. If you find a Web site useful, don't forget to mention its name and address in your work to show that you've used it.

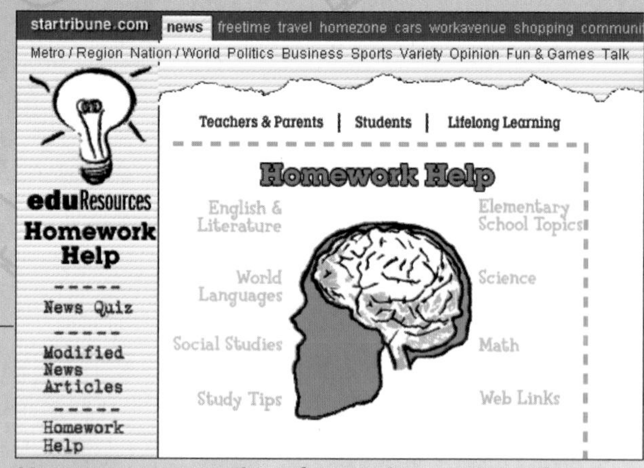

***You can post questions for teachers at* Startribune.**

58 • Ask experts for help

If you're having trouble finding the answer to an important question, you could try asking a teacher or an expert online.

The **Startribune.com Homework Help Web site** has a question-answer service, where you can post questions for teachers to respond to. Before you post a question, you need to make sure that someone else hasn't already asked it.

Click on the category which best fits your query. For example, if you want to know which is the most poisonous creature on Earth, click on the *Science* link on the home page. Next, click on *search* at the bottom of the page, and type in keywords, such as "poisonous" and "creature". You'll see a list of previously asked questions. If none of them answers yours, you can now post your own.

To do this, click on the yellow folder which best fits your question, followed by an appropriate blue discussion point. In this case, it would be *Zoology,* then *Animals*. Scroll down the page, and fill in the online form. Although there is a space to provide your e-mail address, don't enter it. It isn't necessary and it puts your privacy and safety at risk. Finally, click on *Post my message,* and your message will be instantly displayed on the site.

Startribune aims to reply within 24 hours, so check back later to see whether a reply has been posted alongside your question. Don't forget that when you contact teachers or experts for help, they need time to respond. If they're in another country, there may be a time difference of several hours. So don't expect an immediate reply.

59 • Use online educational resources

There are lots of useful educational tools and resources on the Internet. Online encyclopedias are always a good place to start with any research. Some online encyclopedias also have pictures, sounds and other interactive features. At the **Xrefer Web site**, you can search over 50 well-known resources, including various encyclopedias, dictionaries and thesauri.

The **Learning alive Web site** and the **Big chalk site** are two good places to find help with your school work. You can either use their search engines to find information on a topic, or you can browse by subject. The **BBC Web site** also has an excellent study section, organized by age group and subject. When you reach stressful exam times, you'll find their revision guide helpful.

The* BBC Web site*'s Schools page (left) and the* Big Chalk Web site *(right) are good homework sites.

60 • Add clip art to your work

You can make your work look much more impressive and professional by decorating it with clip art, diagrams and charts copied from Web sites. (Again, remember to mention the site they came from in your work.)

There are literally hundreds of free clip art sites on the Internet. You could try doing a keyword search, using the keywords **"clip art"**. The **Discovery School Web site** has a fun clip art gallery which you can browse. Alternatively, if you come across a useful chart or diagram, while researching a topic on the Internet, you can save it and use it in your work.

Right-click on the diagram or clip art picture and select *Save Picture as...* Type a title in the "File name" box, and give it a *.bmp* ending. This means that it will be saved as a "bitmap" picture which can be opened in *Microsoft®* programs, such as *Word* or *Paint*. (Both come free with *Microsoft® Windows® 98*.)

So, for example, if it was a diagram of the inside of a submarine, you could name it: "submarine diagram.bmp". Save it in your *Projects* folder (see page 7), so that you can find it easily later.

How to insert a picture from your* Projects *folder into a* Word *document.

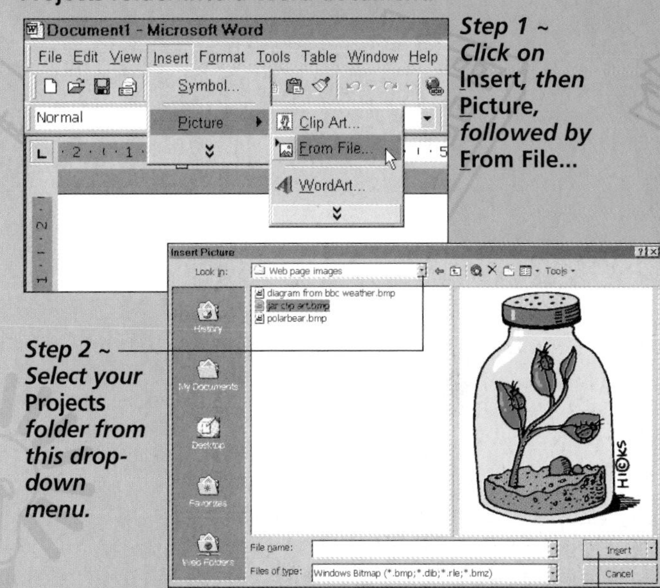

***Step 1 ~ Click on* Insert, *then* Picture, *followed by* From File...**

Step 2 ~ Select your* Projects *folder from this drop-down menu.

***Step 3 ~ Select your picture, then click on* Insert.**

If you'd like to insert the picture into a project which you've typed in *Word*, open your *Word* document and position the flashing cursor where you want it to appear. Click on *Insert*, select *Picture*, and choose *From File...* You now need to browse for the bitmap image which you stored in your *Projects* folder (see step 2 above). Once you have found it, click on *Insert* and it should appear in your document.

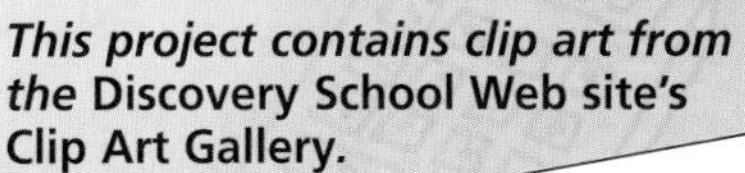

***This project contains clip art from the* Discovery School Web site's Clip Art Gallery.**

Emma Helbrough
Summer Science Project 2002

Exploring Photosynthesis

For my research project, I have chosen to investigate photosynthesis.

Photosynthesis is the scientific process plants use to turn chemicals into food. They absorb sunlight and carbon dioxide through the surface of their leaves, and water through their roots from the surrounding soil.

The carbon dioxide combines with the water, using energy from the sunlight. This produces chemicals called carbohydrates (the plant's food) and also oxygen.

Carbon dioxide
+ Water
+ Energy (sunlight)
Carbohydrates
+ Oxygen

To prove that sunlight is necessary for photosynthesis to take place, I performed a simple experiment. I wrapped a piece of foil around the leaf of a houseplant and secured it with a paper clip. I left it in a sunny place for four days and then removed the foil.

When I removed the foil, I found that the area which had been covered was now ...llow, while the rest of the leaf remained ... that without sunlight, the ...

Lots of Usborne books contain diagrams and pictures like these, which you can download from the Usborne Web site and use in your homework projects.

Exploring space

Your travels on the Internet can reach as far as other galaxies. From the safety of your computer, you can explore deep space, tour Mars, look at far-flung galaxies, and join a space project.

61 • See the Earth from space

Have you ever wondered what it might be like to stand on another planet and look at the Earth? At the **NASA/JPL's A Space Library Web site**, you can use their "Solar System Simulator" to see views of the Earth and other planets from any position in the solar system. So, for example, you could see what Venus looks like from Mars, or the Earth from our Moon.

***The* Solar System Simulator Web site**

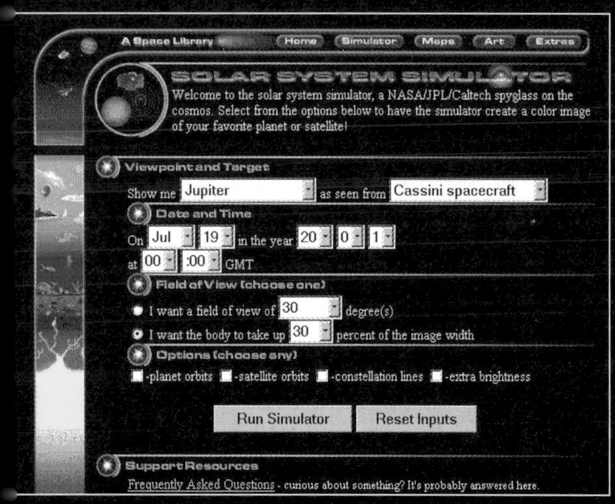

To see a picture, click on *Solar System Simulator* on the Space Library home page. Next, select a planet, or a satellite, and a place to stand from the drop-down menus. Finally, click on *Run Simulator,* and a picture should be displayed.

62 • Explore our solar system

You can explore the planets in our solar system, by going on an interactive virtual tour of space at the **Space.com Web site**. This site has an interactive encyclopedia exploring all the planets in our solar system individually. You'll learn about their size, make-up, position from the Sun, and how they compare with other planets.

You can choose a planet to look at, as well as which parts of the presentation you would like to watch, so you are in complete control of the video. Before you can see the video, you'll need to download the *Macromedia® Flash™* plug-in. (See projects 7 and 8.) Don't forget to turn on your speakers, or you'll miss out on a musical guided tour. Space.com also has an excellent range of video clips on space. Click on *Photos/Videos,* then *Multimedia* for a full list.

A still from* Space.com's *virtual tour of space

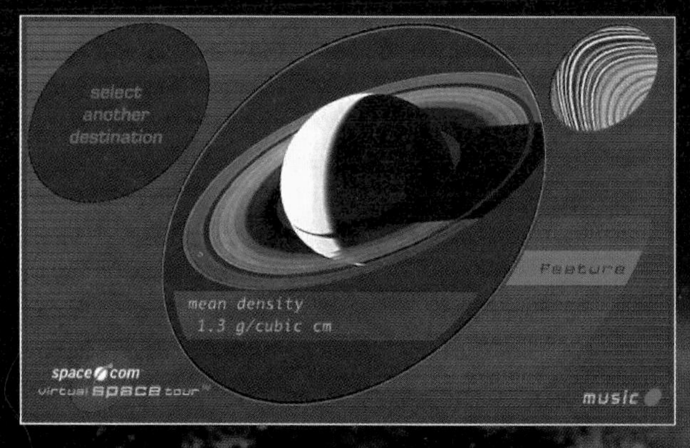

63 • Look at pictures from space

There are some really breathtaking photographs of space to see online. The Hubble Space Telescope has been transmitting pictures from Earth's orbit since 1993. You can look at some of the Hubble's best pictures, as well as many other space photos, at **NASA's Image eXchange Web site** (or NIX for short).

From the home page, click on *Browse* to see an archive of space pictures, past and present. Scroll down the page and click on a subject, such as *Saturn,* to see a set of small pictures. These are called "thumbnails". When you click on one, the computer will download a larger version of the image. Web sites with lots of graphics, like NASA's, often use thumbnails to save people from spending a long time downloading images they don't want to see.

Pictures taken by the Hubble Space Telescope from NASA's Image eXchange (NIX)

The Hubble Space Telescope

64 • Send your name to Mars

In 2003 NASA will be launching their next mission to Mars. This will involve sending out two "Mars Rovers" to explore the surface of the planet. The aim is to find out more about the planet's climate and history. You can get involved, and make your name go down in history at the same time, by taking part in the "Send your name to Mars" project.

NASA are collecting names on the **Send your name to Mars Web site**, to put on a disc which will go inside one of the Mars Rovers during its mission. Perhaps it may come into contact with extraterrestrial life.

Mars Exploration Rover-2003 Mi

Participation Certificate

Presented to

Emma Helbrough

On July 19, 2001

Thank you for joining us on this mission of exploratio
compact disc bearing your name will be included in
Exploration Rover-2003 missions that will explore th
search of geologic evidence of water in Mars' past

Together, we will journey into space to discover as
many wonders of our universe.

Dr Edward J. Weiler
Associate Administrator
Office of Space Science

Certificate No 1887573

You can join NASA's next mission to Mars.

Before you sign up for the mission, you can read more about it on the project's Web page. Then, click on *Sign me up,* type in your name and click on *Add my name*. Once you've signed up, you will be given a certificate to show you've taken part in the project, which you can print by clicking on *File* on the menu bar, followed by *Print...* Remember to set your paper to "Landscape", so that it prints correctly. You'll usually find this option by clicking on *Properties...* in the printer menu.

From dinosaurs to the first people

Dinosaurs may have been extinct for thousands of years, but they've made a dramatic comeback on the Internet. There are museum exhibitions to see online, and impressive simulations to watch. You can even bring dinosaurs to life on your computer by downloading a dinosaur screen saver.

65 • Visit a dinosaur museum

There are now so many natural history museums which display their dinosaur exhibits online that it is almost impossible to recommend just one. A good place to start is at the **Smithsonian Natural History Museum Web site**'s Dinosaur Exhibits page. This museum owns over 1,500 dinosaur exhibits, and you can see around 40 of their best ones on their Web site.

***Here are two of the dinosaur exhibits on the* Smithsonian Natural History Museum Web site.**

To see some of their exhibits, scroll down the Dinosaur Exhibits page, and you will come to a list of choices. There are several ways to view them. You can take a virtual tour of the Museum Hall. Alternatively, you can see an alphabetical list of exhibits, or you can view them by group and time period.

To access the virtual tour, click on *tour the exhibits hall* and then on an exhibit "hot spot" in the picture, to see an enlargement and read more about it.

66 • Watch dinosaur simulations

Computerized animations have brought us closer to picturing the world of dinosaurs than ever before. There are several Web sites on the Internet where you can watch simulations of dinosaurs performing everyday activities, such as walking, eating, hunting and fighting.

The **Discovery Channel Web site** contains some interesting simulations. On the Walking with Dinosaurs page, you can watch several clips from a BBC television series, which explores what the real world of dinosaurs would have been like. (Requires *RealPlayer®* ~ see project 7.) In the Fossil Zone, you can watch robotic animations which explain how a dinosaur's body was structured and how it moved.

***You can watch a simulation of a dinosaur's movements at the* Discovery Channel Web site's Fossil Zone page.**

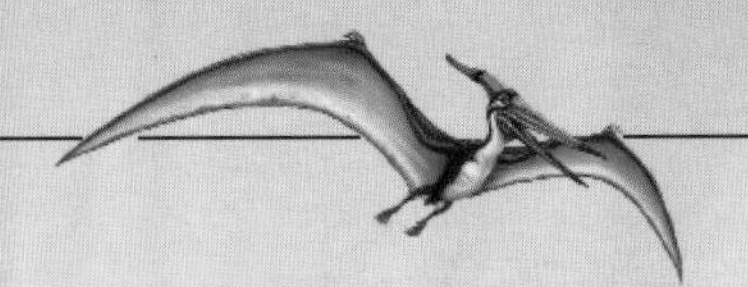

67 • Download a dinosaur screen saver

Screen savers are a great way to personalize your computer, and there are hundreds to download and install for free on the Internet. If you're really into dinosaurs, why not let a group of dinosaurs roam around your screen, like the screen saver on the right?

Alternatively, you could search for a dinosaur-themed screen saver by typing the keywords: **+dinosaur +"screen saver"** (see project 6 for extra help).

Once you have found one you would like to download, click on its download link. Each screen saver will have a different set of steps to follow to download and install it. Use Projects 7-9 for help. (You may need to unzip it, using the instructions provided in project 9.) You can store it in your C drive's *Programs* folder.

To activate the screen saver, go offline and right click on your desktop. A menu will appear. Select *Properties* from the list, and the *Display Properties* window should pop up. Now select the *Screen Saver* tab, and click on the *Screen Saver* drop-down menu to see a list of your system's screen savers. There are normally several to choose from.

Click on the name of the dinosaur screen saver, then click on *OK* to activate it. You can set the exact length of time for the computer to wait before it displays the screen saver in the *Wait* box.

The "Age of Dinosaurs 3D" screen saver lets a group of dinosaurs roam around your computer screen.

This is the* Display Properties *window.

Select the dinosaur screen saver here.

68 • Explore cave paintings

The first people didn't appear until 2 million years ago, which is around 63 million years after the dinosaurs died out.

You can take a virtual tour of some 17,000 year old cave paintings in the south west of France at the **Cave of Lascaux Web site**. This beautifully designed site shows some of the most well-preserved prehistoric cave paintings in the world. Obviously there are no dinosaur pictures to see, but there are lots of mammals, including horses and bulls.

To go on the virtual tour, you'll need to make sure your browser is Java™ enabled (see project 31). Then, select a language on the home page, and click on *discover* followed by *virtual visit.* You can use the clickable map to navigate around the caves.

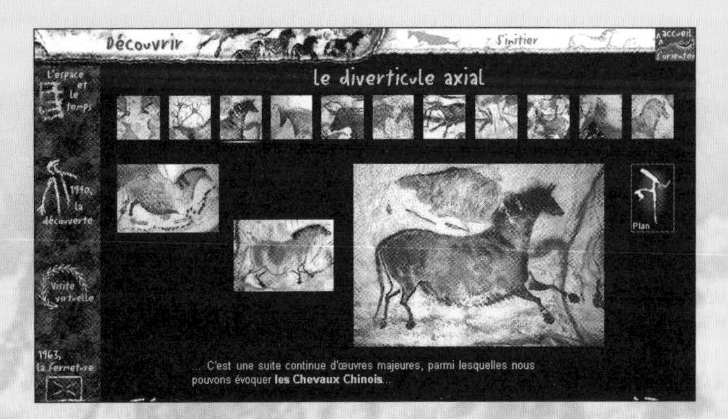

Science

The Internet brings the world of science to life. It's full of fun, interactive activities. You can do online experiments, or watch video clips which explain difficult scientific processes, and you can even try designing your own roller coaster.

At the **Annenberg/CPB Exhibits Web site,** ***you can design your own roller coaster and brush up on your physics along the way.***

69 • Do an experiment

There are lots of sites on the Internet where you can get involved in experiments, or try hands-on activities. Three good Web sites to explore are **Try Science**, **Exploratorium** and the **Annenberg/CPB Exhibits Web site**.

At the **Try Science Web site**, you'll find a whole host of experiments to print and try at home. There are also great links to sites where you'll find more information about the topics covered in the experiments. Try finding out how strong a shark's sense of smell is, or build a rainforest canopy. Click on *experiments* on the home page to access the activities.

There is also a directory of science museums around the world. To find a list of local museums, click on *field trips* on the home page, and select your country from the drop-down menu.

The **Exploratorium Web site** is part of a science, art and human perception museum in San Francisco. This brilliant Web site contains lots of hands-on activities to take part in, such as exploring optical illusions. You'll find a good selection of online activities by clicking on *The Learning Studio,* then *online exhibits.* As this is such an excellent site, it's well worth exploring the rest of it too.

At the **Annenberg/CPB Exhibits Web site** you can try designing your own roller coaster. This doesn't sound all that scientific, but you'll be amazed at how much you learn about physics while doing the project. On the home page, click on *Amusement Park Physics* and get designing.

70 • Watch and learn

Sometimes books just aren't enough help when you're trying to grasp a difficult scientific concept. Visual aids make things a lot clearer. At the **BrainPOP Web site** you'll find a complete directory of entertaining animations, on everything from atoms and relativity to eclipses and rainbows.

The short animations are organized into four categories: *health, science, technology* and *special*. You'll need the *Macromedia®* *Flash™* plug-in (use projects 7 and 8 to help you). Don't forget to turn on your speakers. Once you've watched the movie, try doing the quiz to test your new knowledge.

The* BrainPOP *home page

A still from a* BrainPOP *movie on electromagnetic waves

71 • Read exciting science news

Technical jargon sometimes makes for boring reading. At The **Why Files Web site**, however, you'll find a whole series of entertainingly written scientific articles.

This Web site looks at the science behind current news stories. So the articles are always about issues that are of topical interest.

To access the full range of stories, click on *Archives* on the home page. The articles are arranged in categories, such as *health*, *space* and *the future*, so it's easy to find something to interest you. Many of the articles have links to extra pages of information. This means that you can read as much or as little of each story as you like.

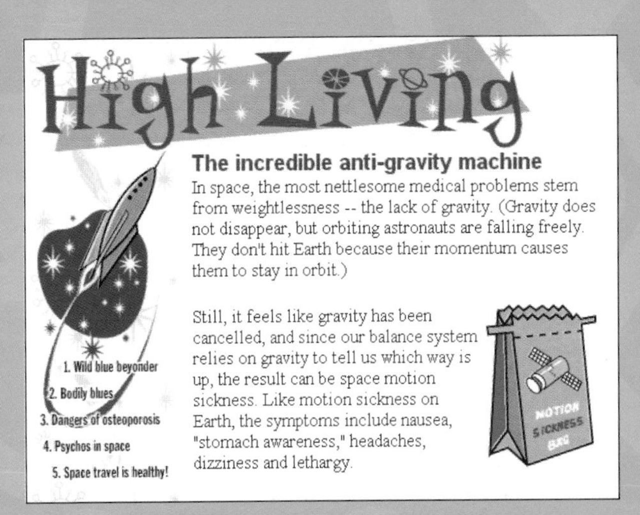

This is an article from the* Why Files *Web site, which discusses how living in space affects astronauts, psychologically and physically.

72 • Explore an interactive periodic table

Even the periodic table has been spiced up on the Internet. The **chemsoc Web site**, hosted by the Royal Society of Chemistry, has an impressive "Visual Elements Periodic Table". The usual element symbols (such as "H" for hydrogen) have been replaced with futuristic, computer-generated images, and each image relates somehow to the element.

If you let the mouse rest over one of these images, the traditional symbol will be displayed in the bottom right-hand corner of the page. Click on an element, to learn about its properties, uses and history. (For more detailed information, click on *html* on this page.) You'll also find an explanation of what the new image is and why it has been chosen. This site is best viewed using the *Macromedia® Shockwave®* plug-in, so if you haven't already downloaded it, you can do so through a link on the site. (Use projects 7 and 8 to help you.)

You can view* chemsoc's *"Visual Elements Periodic Table" online. Click on a symbol for more information.

Click on this gold symbol, at any point, to return to the periodic table.

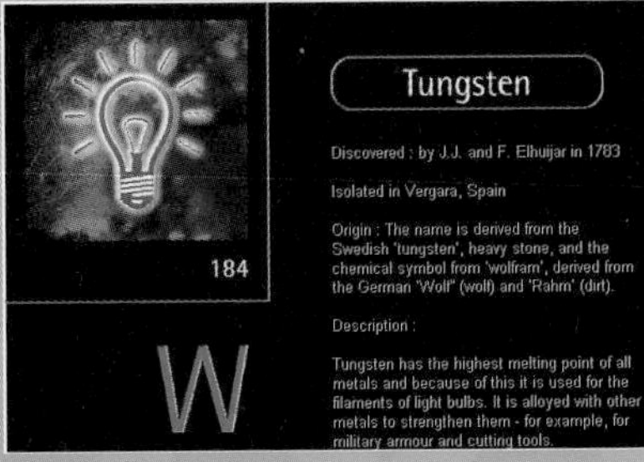

A light bulb symbol is used to represent the element tungsten, because it is used in the production of light bulbs.

History

The Internet provides a gateway to exploring past times and ancient cultures, so you can use it to piece together a picture of the past. There are simulations of ancient buildings to view, as well as many amazing historical objects from around the world, such as the 900-year-old Bayeux Tapestry.

Lots of people use the Internet to trace their own family history and there are hundreds of sites which can help you to do this. Who knows, you may even discover a distant famous connection in your family.

A "still" from the animated version of the Bellerophon myth at the **Mythweb Web site**

73 • Read an animated myth

Although they are a few thousand years old, Greek myths are still some of the most exciting stories ever written.

The **Mythweb Web site** has developed illustrated versions of some of the most popular stories, about heroes such as Hercules and Theseus, and they are retold in a funny and entertaining way.

One particular myth, about a hero called Bellerophon, who rode through the skies on a winged horse named *Pegasus*, is brought to life with animated illustrations. To read this particular story, click on *Heroes* on the home page and then select *Bellerophon.* Click on *Bellerophon* again on the next page to reach the start of the story. Use the arrows at the top of each page to turn the pages.

74 • See the Seven Wonders of the World

Scholars in Ancient Greece wrote about the incredible monuments of their time, which they named "the Seven Wonders of the Ancient World". These included: *the Pharos of Alexandria*, an enormous lighthouse which acted as a beacon for ships sailing into the port; *the Statue of Zeus at Olympia* and *the Hanging Gardens of Babylon.* The only one to survive is *the Great Pyramid at Giza,* in Egypt. You have to use your imagination to picture the others.

At the **PBS Nova Online site**, you can use your detective skills to untangle the clues to decide which description matches each Wonder. In each case, you'll be given a science, history and geography clue. When you get a right answer, you'll be rewarded with a beautiful illustration of how they might have looked.

The Great Pyramid is the only surviving Wonder of the Seven Wonders of the World.

75 • View the Bayeux Tapestry

The Norman Conquest of England in 1066 was an important event in European history. William the Conqueror seized the English throne, following his victory over Harold of Wessex at the Battle of Hastings. It is believed that Harold died during the battle from an arrow through his eye. Shortly afterwards, the whole saga, including Harold's sticky end, was hand-stitched as an enormous 70m (231ft) long tapestry, known as the Bayeux Tapestry.

Amazingly, this 900 year old tapestry has survived to the present day and you can view it, section-by-section, at the **Osprey Essential Norman Conquest site**. You'll need the *Macromedia® Shockwave®* plug-in to see it ~ use projects 7 and 8 for help. Read the instructions, then click on *Version for Windows*. Use the arrows to scroll along the tapestry.

A section of the Bayeux Tapestry

Some people create personal Web pages to display their family history findings.

76 • Trace your family roots

Some people know a lot about their family history, while others know very little. Studying family histories is known as genealogy. Through the Internet, it is becoming a very popular hobby. Some genealogists have traced their roots back over hundreds of years using record offices which you can access online.

If you're interested in building your own family tree, a good place to start is the **Genealogy Spot Web site**, which has a huge list of links. Those who are new to genealogy can click on *For beginners* or *For kids,* where you'll find links to online tutorials on how to get started. There are also links to sites where you can search public records. Some search engines allow you to narrow down the field with categories such as *country* and *ethnicity*.

Genealogy can be a very time-consuming hobby, and it may take a lot of hard work to find what you're looking for, so try to be patient. You may even discover a close living relative that you didn't know about before.

Museums and galleries

Many museums and galleries have excellent Web sites, designed to advertise their collections, and to give access to art, culture and history for those who aren't able to visit them in person.

77 • Find an online exhibition

A good place to start if you're interested in looking at museum exhibits online is the **WWW Virtual Library: Museums around the World Web site**. It has links to hundreds of museum Web pages, which are listed by country. Alternatively, the **MuseumSpot Web site** is very well organized and guides you around museums with the best online exhibitions and activities. Below are a selection of museum and gallery sites you might like to visit.

The State Hermitage Museum in St Petersburg, Russia, has an excellent Web site. Go on a virtual tour to explore it fully.

78 • Go on an art safari

Sometimes you need a little guidance when looking at exhibits on a museum Web site, just as you would get if you visited the real museum.

You can enhance your visit to the **Museum of Modern Art Web site** by going on their art safari. This helps you to explore the paintings in more detail and think about why the artist painted them and what he or she was trying to achieve.

You'll find another similar activity at the (American) **National Museum of Wildlife Art: Art Tales Web site**, although this time you become the museum curator. You have to design your own exhibition about a particular artist or theme. From the Art Tales home page, click on *Museum Curator* and read the instruction. Now click on *Let's begin*. Select eight wildlife pictures which relate to your chosen theme, scroll down the page and click on *Okay*.

You need to write a short piece to accompany each exhibit. Describe what you think is going on in the picture, why the artist might have painted it, and how it makes you feel. You can then publish your exhibition on their Web site.

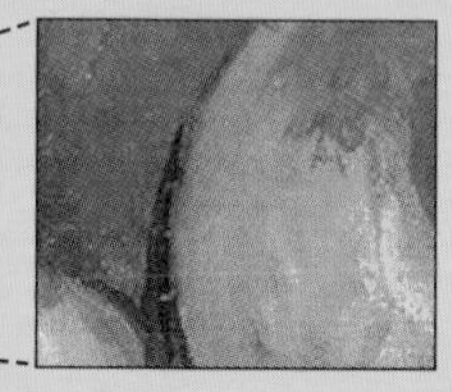

You can zoom in on any area of a picture from the museum's digital collection for a closer look at the detailed brush work.

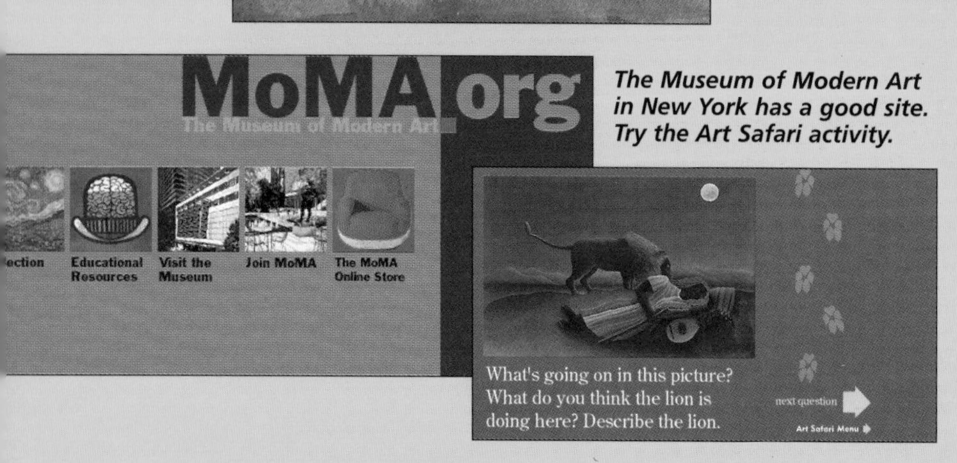

The Museum of Modern Art in New York has a good site. Try the Art Safari activity.

Visit Ancient Egypt at the British Museum in London's Web site.

79 • Have your picture published

The **Worldwide Kid's Art Gallery Web site** displays pictures by young artists. You can submit artwork which has been drawn on paper, or on a computer, using a drawing program such as *Microsoft® Paint*.

To turn artwork drawn on paper into a computer file, you need to use a machine called a scanner (see page 7). Art sites usually contain clear instructions on how to submit pictures. They normally state what resolution your pictures should be. Most pictures on the Internet have a low resolution of 75 dpi.

When you have scanned a picture, use the imaging software to save it as a GIF or JPEG file. These are the file formats most commonly used for Web images. Once you have submitted a picture, return to the site a couple of days later to see whether your picture has been displayed.

Two pictures from the **Worldwide Kid's Art Gallery**

"Reds", painted by Chelsea Isbister from Canada

Nevena Vereski, from Yugoslavia, created her picture using **Microsoft® Paint.**

80 • Get some art wallpaper

As you explore museums and galleries online, you may come across a picture you particularly like. You could use this to decorate your desktop. A picture or pattern that covers your desktop is called wallpaper.

To use a picture from a Web site as your wallpaper, wait until the picture has completely downloaded, then click on it with your right mouse button. From the menu which appears, select *Set As Wallpaper*. When you close your browser, and any other open programs, you will see the picture on your desktop.

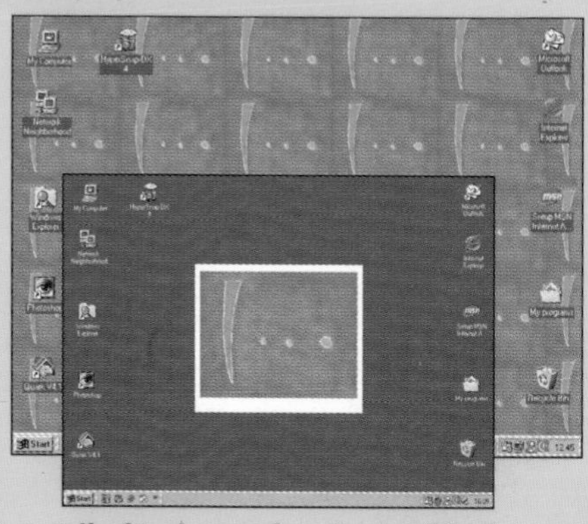

A "tiled" picture (at the back) and a "centered" picture (at the front)

If you want to change the way the picture is displayed, close any programs you have open, and right click with your mouse on the desktop. From the menu that appears, select *Properties,* and the *Display Properties* dialog box will appear. Click on the *Background* tab. There are three ways to display your wallpaper. You can select *Center* to see the picture in the middle of the page, *Tile* to see it repeated, or *Stretch* to make it cover your desktop. Finally, click on *OK* to finish.

You can see the Water Gardens Monet painted at the **Montreal Museum of Fine Arts Web site.**

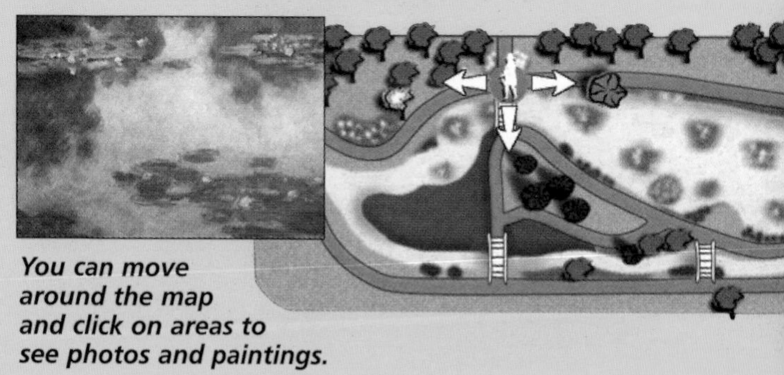

You can move around the map and click on areas to see photos and paintings.

Planning days out

Although the Internet gives you access to information about the whole world, you can also use it to find out about your local area. If you're planning a day out, you can find out what's on, book tickets and plan your journey.

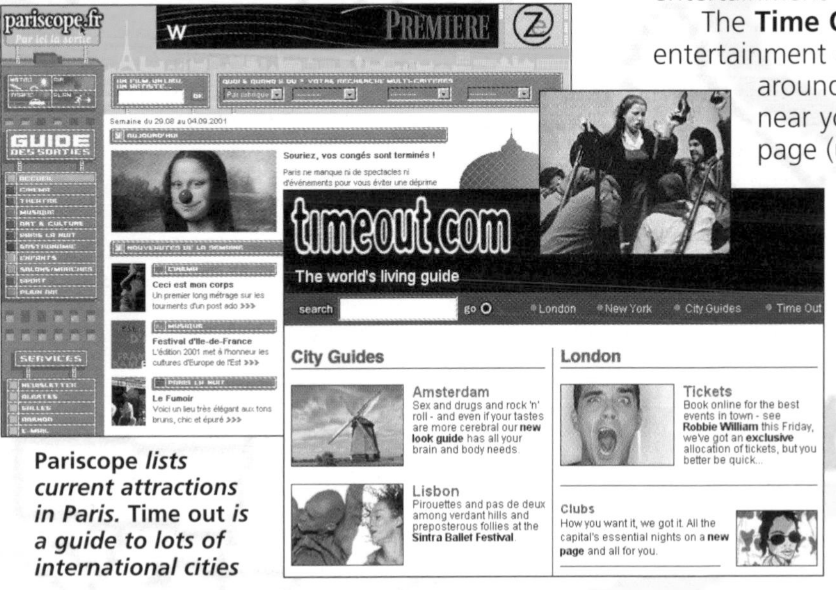

Pariscope *lists current attractions in Paris.* **Time out** *is a guide to lots of international cities*

81 • Find out what's on

You can find out about current events in your area, including exhibitions, plays, concerts and other attractions, by reading an online entertainment guide.

The **Time Out Web site** has an entertainment guide for over 30 major cities around the world. To find out what's on near you, click on a city from the home page (under "City Guides"). Each city guide has current reviews of everything from local restaurants to sporting events.

The **Virgin.net Web site** has some great ideas for days out in the U.K.. You can use their "Day out finder" search engine for a quick way of finding things to do. Type in a place and choose a subject, such as *Theme Parks and Attractions,* then click on *Go.* A list of ideas should be displayed.

82 • Book tickets online for an event

If you're planning to go to a music concert, sporting event, or an exhibition, you can book tickets in advance online.

The **Ticketmaster Web site** provides an online booking service for events in several countries around the world. To purchase tickets, browse for an event using the directory on the home page. If, for example, you wanted to book a ticket for a music concert, click on a music style, such as *Rock & Pop*, and browse through the event list. Alternatively you can use the search engine to see if a band is listed.

Each event listed on the site will have information about the city, venue, time and date it is being held. You can click on the name of a venue to find out exactly where it is. (Make sure you choose one that isn't too far away.)

Once you have chosen a concert, click on the band's name next to the correct date and venue. On the next page, click on *On Sale* under "Buy". Pages 32-33 explain how to pay for things online. If you're under 18, you may need to ask someone who is for help.

You can use the **Ticketmaster Web site** *to buy tickets online for events such as WOMAD, the world of music, arts and dance festival.*

83 • Get a train timetable

If your day out involves a train journey, you might find it useful to download and print a train timetable to take with you.

Lots of rail companies display timetables online and some provide details of fares and online booking services. Try using the **Ask web site** to find a local timetable. Type in the question **Where can I find a train timetable?**

At the **Railtrack Web site**, there is a search engine which simplifies planning train journeys in the U.K.. Type in your departure station, arrival station and then the date and time of travel. The search will produce a list of possible trains and routes. Each route will have details of how long it should take, and how many changes you will need to make. The **Amtrak Web site** provides a similar service for planning train journeys across the U.S.A. Just fill in the "Fast Fare Finder" form on the Trains and Destinations page for a list of times, routes and fares.

84 • Use street maps to plan your journeys

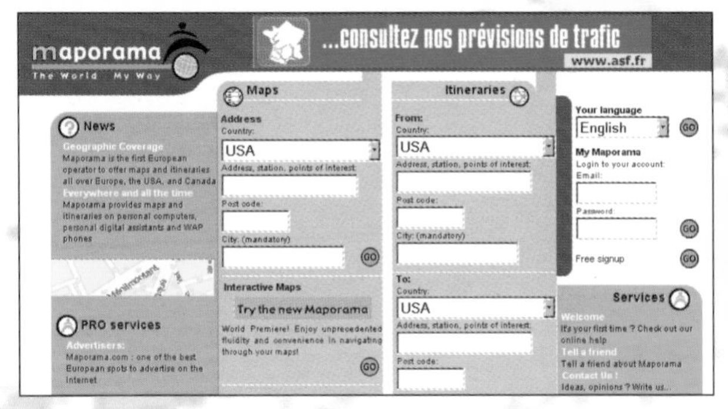

The **Maporama** *home page*

One really useful service that the Internet provides is online maps. These are much easier to use than traditional maps. You can zoom in and out for a clearer picture, and you can print a copy, to take with you on your journey.

The **Maporama Web site** has very detailed maps of Europe, the U.S.A. and Canada. To find a map, click on the *Interactive Maps* section, select a country from the drop-down menu and enter a place name, or a postal (zip) code. Then, click *go.* A map should be displayed. You can zoom in and out by using the **+** and **-** symbols just below the map. Try typing in your own postal code to produce a map of your street.

You can also use Maporama to plan car journeys. On the home page, fill in the form under 'Itineraries'. Enter a starting address and a destination address. Click on *go*. A map and a guide on how to get there should be displayed.

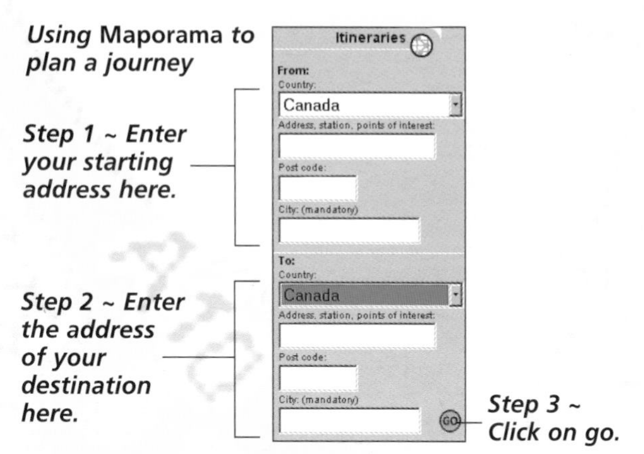

Step 4 ~ A map and a route guide will be downloaded.

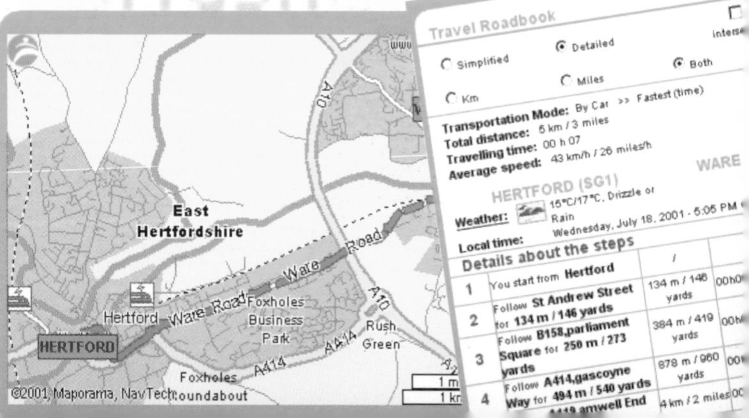

Travel and tourism

The Internet is very useful for planning trips. You can find out about destinations, plan which sights to see, book your flight and brush up on the local language. If you aren't planning a trip for a while, you can go on a virtual visit instead.

***The One World Journeys site** combines great photography and travel reports.*

85 • Find tourist information

If you're planning a trip abroad, you might like some help choosing a destination. The **World Travel Guide Web site** has lots of tourist information about places around the world.

To find some information about Thailand, for example, visit the World Travel Guide home page and click on *South East Asia* on the world map. A map of South East Asia will download. Now, click on *Thailand.* You'll be taken to a page which gives a brief description of the destination. For more detailed information, click on a topic, such as *Beaches*, from the list on the right of the page.

You can use the Internet to research the local language and currency of your destination. The **E-Conflict™ World Encyclopedia Web site** has lots of useful information about many countries, including details about their history and economy. To find out more, select a country from the drop-down menu on the home page.

86 • Go on a virtual trip

If you're not planning a trip in the near future, you can go on a virtual visit instead. There are several ways to do this. Some sites, such as the **National Geographic site** and the **One World Journeys site**, have amazing photographs, video clips and travel reports. At other sites, you can see pictures which rotate 360 degrees, to give you a real impression of what places look like. These are called panoramic pictures.

The **American Express® Web site** has over 50 panoramic pictures of famous sights around the world. (Your browser needs to be "Java-enabled" in order to see the panaromic pictures on this site. See project 31 for help.) You can also follow explorers on real-life adventures. The **Goals Web site** has reports and photos from explorers taking part in some amazing journeys, such as an attempt at rowing around the world.

*At the **American Express Web site**, you can see amazing travel photos that rotate 360 degrees.*

87 • Find and book a flight

Once you've decided on the destination for your trip, you may need to find and book a flight. You can do this over the Internet. Most flight companies provide online booking services and timetables for flights all over the world.

The **Air France Web site** offers both of these services on its Web site. To see a timetable, first select your country on the home page. Then, click on the *schedules* link, and type in the airport you will be departing from, your chosen destination and a possible date for travel. A page showing a timetable of flights will appear. You can find out about how to book flights by clicking on the *Booking online* link.

The Air France *home page*

88 • Learn some travel phrases

If you're visiting a country where your native language isn't spoken, you could learn some basic travel phrases before you go. The Internet has lots of language learning resources. If you're not a beginner, you'll find there are more advanced lessons too.

You can learn some basic travel phrases for over 80 languages at the **TravelLang Web site**. Scroll down the page and select your own language from the drop-down menu. Next, click on the language you would like to learn from the selection below. On the next page, select a topic, such as *Basic words* or *Directions,* and a list of phrases will be displayed. If you switch on your speakers and click on a phrase, you can listen to how it is pronounced. Another useful tool for any language student is an online dictionary. The **YourDictionary.com Web site** has online dictionaries in over 250 languages.

89 • Plan an action adventure

Most travel sites provide information on ordinary sight-seeing trips. But what if you're looking for an action-packed adventure? You could try visiting the **FunAdventure.com Web site**. This site has gathered together details of exciting activities around the world. So, whether you want to go paragliding in Africa, whitewater-rafting in Costa Rica, or trekking around the North Pole, you can organize it here.

Once you have chosen an adventure, scroll down to the bottom of the description page, and you'll see an online form. This form will put you in touch with the organizers of your chosen activity. You need to fill in the form, providing your contact details and an idea of when you'd like to go. It will then be passed on to the organizers, who will send you some information about the trip. Alternatively, you could just use this site to think of ideas for activities to take part in on your next trip away somewhere.

These pictures, from the* FunAdventure Web site, *show some of the activities on offer.

The news and weather

The Internet is fast becoming one of the most popular places to find the latest news. You can access stories about any country, in any language, wherever you are in the world and you can read them almost as soon as they break.

The **La Stampa Web site** ***has the latest news in Italian.***

90 • Get the latest news

A good place to find an online newspaper to suit you is the **News and Newspapers Online Service Web site**. This site has extensive links to online newspapers around the world. Click on a country, or state, for a list of suitable online news links and a description of what topics they cover.

Most online newspapers display the latest news on their home page and have an archive which you can search for past articles. Sometimes you can sign up to receive news updates by e-mail, as part of a one-way mailing list (i.e. you can't reply to the messages).

One news site which offers this service is the **Ananova Web site**. You can register to receive updates on stories that interest you.

To sign up, click on *alerts* on the home page. Then click on *choose some subjects,* and the full catalogue will be displayed. Select a topic, such as "celebrities", and tick the box next to any stories of interest, then click *Sign up now.* On the next page, fill in the online form and click *register.* You can add or remove stories at any time by revisiting the *alerts* page and clicking on *Sign in here.*

The AFP site has news pages in English, French, German, Spanish and Portuguese.

The ABC News Web site ***has thorough coverage of the U.S.A.***

You can watch the news, read by a computer-generated newsreader, at the **Ananova Web site.** ***(Requires*** **RealPlayer®** ***.)***

91 • Write for an online newspaper

Why not contribute to a Web magazine (or e-zine) that is created by people from all over the world? If you have written an article and would like to get it published online, you can send it to the **Yomag.net Web site**, an online newspaper written by young writers, for young people. They publish articles on a wide range of topics, including sports, movies and music.

If you would like to write for yomag.net, visit their site first and look at other young writers' articles, then send your own article by e-mail to: **webmaster@yomag.net**. If you get more than three articles published, you'll receive a certificate and you'll get the chance to attend a yomag.net editorial meeting.

92 • Work with the news

You may find a news story on the Internet which is relevant to a piece of work you're doing. It's easy to copy text from a Web page into a word processing program and insert it into an essay or project. First, save all the text on the Web page by selecting *Save As* from the *File* menu. In the *Save as type* box, select *Text file*, and change the ending of the filename from *.html* to *.txt*. Click on *Save*.

Go offline, close your browser, and open a word processing program, such as *Microsoft® Word*. Select *File* then *Open*, and browse to find the document you saved. You will see the text from the Web page. You may need to delete any extra text which has been copied from the page along with your article, such as advertisements. You can change how the text looks and you can copy a section of it to use as a quote by highlighting it and using the *Copy* and *Paste* commands in your word processing program's *Edit* menu. If you copy text from a Web site in this way, ensure that you make it clear that it is not your own work. You should also state where you found the information.

***An article from* Yahoo! news**

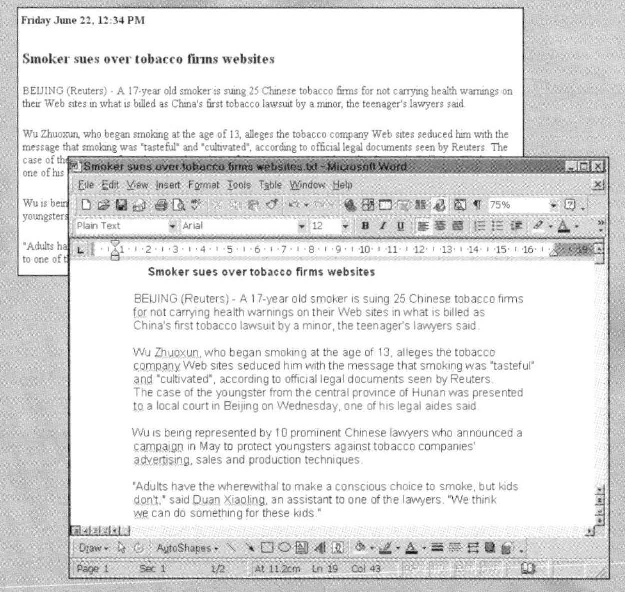

Friday June 22, 12:34 PM

Smoker sues over tobacco firms websites

BEIJING (Reuters) - A 17-year old smoker is suing 25 Chinese tobacco firms for not carrying health warnings on their Web sites in what is billed as China's first tobacco lawsuit by a minor, the teenager's lawyers said.

Wu Zhuoxun, who began smoking at the age of 13, alleges the tobacco company Web sites seduced him with the message that smoking was "tasteful" and "cultivated", according to official legal documents seen by Reuters. The case of th...

Smoker sues over tobacco firms websites.txt - Microsoft Word

Smoker sues over tobacco firms websites

BEIJING (Reuters) - A 17-year old smoker is suing 25 Chinese tobacco firms for not carrying health warnings on their Web sites in what is billed as China's first tobacco lawsuit by a minor, the teenager's lawyers said.

Wu Zhuoxun, who began smoking at the age of 13, alleges the tobacco company Web sites seduced him with the message that smoking was "tasteful" and "cultivated", according to official legal documents seen by Reuters. The case of the youngster from the central province of Hunan was presented to a local court in Beijing on Wednesday, one of his legal aides said.

Wu is being represented by 10 prominent Chinese lawyers who announced a campaign in May to protect youngsters against tobacco companies' advertising, sales and production techniques.

"Adults have the wherewithal to make a conscious choice to smoke, but kids don't," said Duan Xiaoling, an assistant to one of the lawyers. "We think we can do something for these kids."

The text from the page above has been copied into a word processing program.

93 • Read a weather report

Another useful online service that many sites provide is weather reports. These are particularly useful when planning days out, or for finding out what the weather is going to be like at your travel destination. The **BBC Web site** has a good section on the weather, with regional, national and international forecasts. You can look at a daily forecast, or get a report on the week ahead.

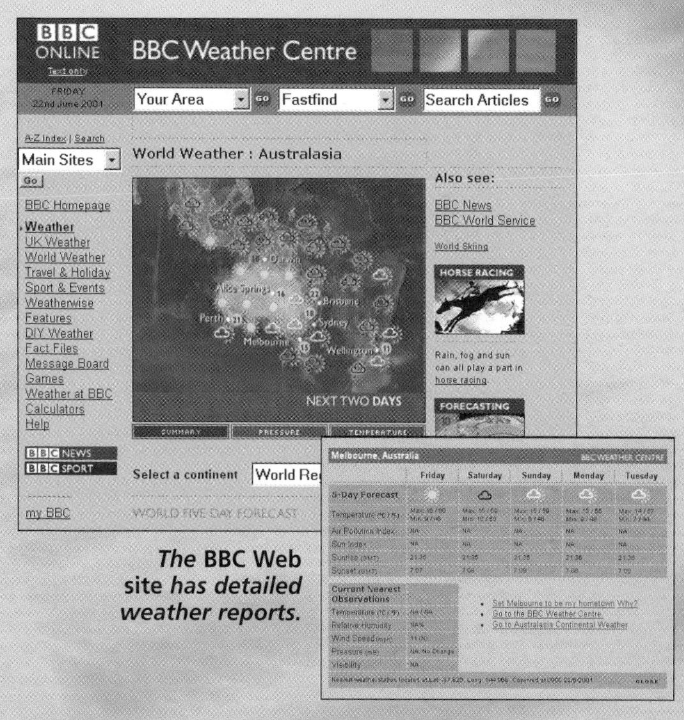

The* BBC Web *site has detailed weather reports.

As well as the latest reports, there are also educational sections on the science behind it all, and games with a weather theme. You can find out what it is like to be a weather presenter, using the interactive weather map.

Design your own Web page

Although Web pages look very complicated to produce, they're actually suprisingly easy. You could design a Web site about a sport, hobby, or band, or you could create a site about a local club you belong to.

There are two different ways to design Web pages. You can use a a Web editor program, such as *Microsoft® FrontPage®*, or a special code called HTML. Projects 94-101 show how to make a Web page, step-by-step, using HTML.

Try visiting some personal Web sites to get ideas for your own site.

94 • Get started with HTML

HTML is the basic code behind all Web page design, so it is a good idea to learn how to use it. If you do go on to use a Web editor program, you will find it much easier if you already understand how HTML works.

HTML is basically a set of instructions which tell a browser what to show on a Web page and how to show it. You don't need a special program to make a Web page using HTML. You can use a simple editing program, such as *Microsoft® Notepad*, which comes free with *Windows*. To open *Notepad*, click on the *Start* menu in the corner of your desktop. Select *Programs* and, from the menu which appears, click on *Accessories*. Finally, click on *Notepad*.

On the blank page that appears, you are going to write your set of instructions in HTML code. These instructions are called "tags" and each tag has brackets around it. Tags come in pairs and work rather like quotation marks. There are opening tags, which look **<like this>**, and closing tags, which look **</like this>**. (Notice that closing tags have a slash after the first bracket.)

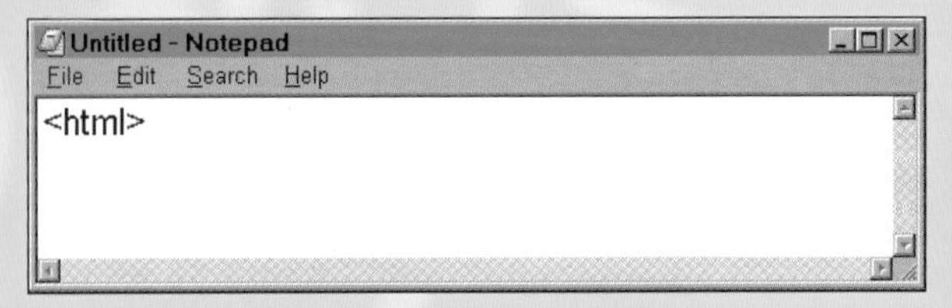

***Adding the first HTML tag to a Web page in* Notepad**

The very first tag tells your browser that the page is going to be written in HTML. This won't show on your Web page. Write the tag as **<html>**.

95 • Add the head

Web pages contain two sections: the "head" and the "body". The head contains information about the page which won't actually appear on it, such as its title, and the body contains the features which you see on the page, such as the text and pictures.

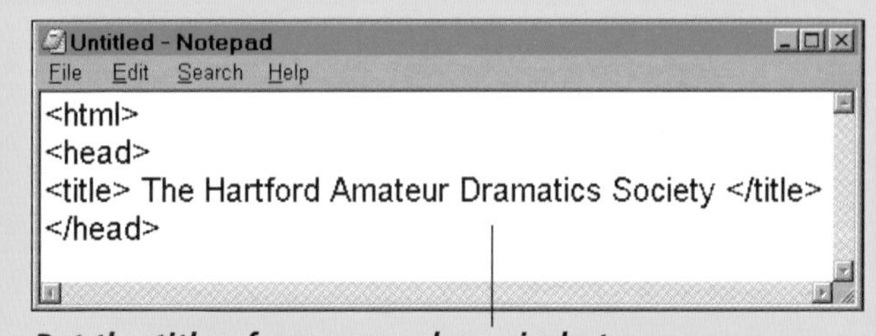

Put the title of your page here, in-between the two tags: <title> and </title>.

You need to add the head first. Press *Return* after <html>. Then, begin with the opening tag: **<head>**. Again, press *Return,* and add another opening tag **<title>**, to introduce the official title of your Web page. (This will not appear on the page, but will help to identify it later.) Next to the tag, type in your title, and add the closing tag **</title>**, as shown above. Finally, press *Return*, and close the head using the tag **</head>**. This may seem a little fiddly at first, but you'll get used to the code fairly quickly.

96 • Add text to the body

Once you've finished the head, you can begin constructing the body of your page. As well as typing the text you'd like to appear, you can also type instructions about how you want it to look, including the style, size and position of the text.

Press *Return* after the head's closing tag, and add the opening tag **<body>**. Now add a page heading. You can make it appear across the middle of your page by adding the opening and closing tags **<center>** and **</center>** around it. Headings come in six letter sizes: h1, h2, h3, h4, h5 and h6. H1 is the largest and h1-h3 are used most often. Choose a size and add the tags, such as **<h1>** and **</h1>**, around your heading. It should now look something like this:

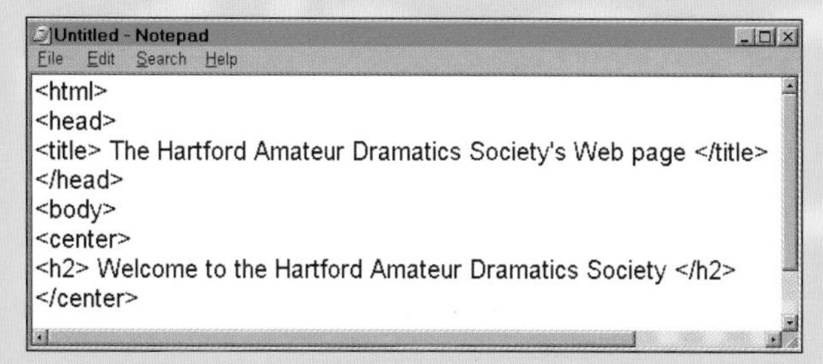

The page's heading appears in-between two pairs of tags: <center> <h2> the heading </h2> </center>.

Next, add the main section of your text. You need to choose the text size, which is on a scale of 1-7, but this time 1 is the smallest and 7 is the largest. Choose a size and type it into the tag, as follows: **<font size = 4>**. Type in your text, separating each paragraph with the tag **<p>**. (You don't need to add a closing tag for this command.)

When you've entered all the text, add the closing tag **</font size = 4>**. Press *Return* and add the closing body tag **</body>**. Press *Return* again, and finish by adding the closing tag **</html>**. Your page should now look like this:

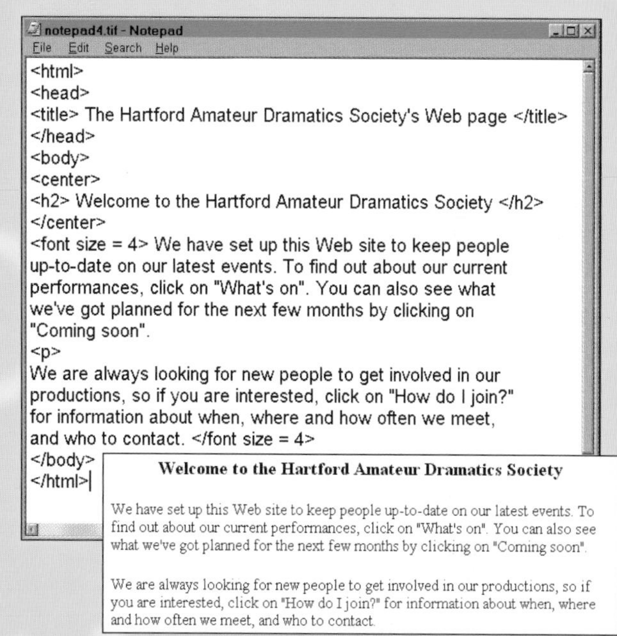

You can check how your Web page looks by saving it as an HTML file (see project 97 below).

97 • See how it looks so far

You can see how your page looks at any stage, by saving it as an HTML file. To do this, you need to add the finishing tags **</body>** and **</html>** (you can remove them again later) and then click on *File* followed by *Save*. A dialog box will appear. In the *Save in* menu, select the *Projects* folder (see page 7). Give it a filename and add the ending *.html*, so it should look something like this: *My Web page.html*. Now click on *Save*.

My Web page.html

Look for this icon in your Projects folder.

Close *Notepad*, click on your *Projects* folder on the desktop, followed by your HTML file.

Your browser will open onto the Web page. This does not mean that it is now connected to the World Wide Web. Project 101 shows you how to put it on the Web once it is complete. For now, it will just be useful to see how it looks. You can then go back and add more features or change the style of one of the elements.

To make any changes, you will have to open the file while you are in *Notepad*. Click on *File*, then *Open...* Make sure you select *All files* from the *Files of type* menu just below the *File name* box. Browse for your *Projects* folder in the *Look in* menu and then click on your HTML file.

98 • *Create some hyperlinks*

You can link your Web page to any other page on the Internet using a hyperlink (or link). These are useful for helping visitors to find out more about the subject of your page. For example, if your page includes some information about the pop star Madonna, you could create a hyperlink to her record company's site, or to a page where you can listen to her songs.

Alison also has a Web page.

A hyperlink

For more tips on drawing cartoons, try visiting these links:

Emmett Scott's Cartoon Corner
Slylock Fox's drawing lessons
Cartoon connection
Doodlematic

If your site was about drawing cartoons, you might like to add links to some similar useful sites.

To add a hyperlink, you can use a tag called an anchor tag. This will instruct your browser to go to another page and tell it where the page's information is stored. First, you need to find the URL of the page you want to link to. Next, decide which words you want to use as the link. So, if you want to link to a friend's Web page, you can use his or her name as the link.

An opening anchor tag looks something like this: **<a href="?">**, except you need to replace the question mark with the URL of the site you are linking to. After the tag, type in the words you want to use to represent the URL. Finally, add the closing tag **</a>**. Here is an example: **<a hef="www.alison.net"> Alison </a>**. This would appear on the Web page as **Alison**, as shown in the picture above, left.

You can tell if a picture or a piece of text is a hyperlink by passing your mouse over it. Your mouse pointer will turn into a hand pointer when it rests over a hyperlink.

99 • *Add a background*

Once you have entered your text, as shown in projects 94-98, you can start to add design features to your page. Adding a background will make it bright and fun. There are two ways to add a background. You can add a picture, which will appear as a tiled pattern across the whole of the page, or you can just make the page a different shade. If you use a picture for a background, try to keep it simple, and make sure you can still read the text on your page.

In HTML, each shade has a special six figure code, called a hex code. **CCFFFF** is the code for pale blue, for example, and **000088** produces dark blue. There is a useful selection of codes below. When you have selected one, you need to insert the code into your opening body tag (which you added in project 96), as follows: **<body bgcolor= CCFFFF>**. There is no need to add the code to the closing body tag.

Background pictures are also added as part of the opening body tag. Instead of writing a hex code, you need to add the picture's filename, so that your browser can find it and download it. Add the filename to the opening body code as follows: **<body background= "polar bear.jpg">**.

You'll need to save background and foreground images (see project 100) as GIF or JPEG files, as these are the file formats used for pictures on Web sites. (Project 79 shows you how to scan and save images.) Save photographs as JPEGs by adding the ending *.jpg after* the filename, and save cartoons and simple pictures as GIFs by adding *.gif.*

#000000 #000088 #0000FF #FF00FF #008800 #00FF00 #00FFFF #880000 #FF0000 #FFFF00 #FFFFFF

100 • Add pictures and photos

If the site is about your own band you could add a picture of the group.

You can add photographs and other pictures to decorate your Web page, or you can use them as a way of presenting information. For example, you could use one to show a sports team you play for, or a band you belong to.

To add a photograph to the foreground, you need to save it as a JPEG (see project 99). Then, you need to help your browser find where it is stored on your computer, by adding the filename as part of the next tag. Insert the tag **<img src="polar bear.jpg">**, replacing the words *polar bear.jpg* with your picture's filename. You also need to state how big you want your foreground image to be. You can give measurements in pixels (see page 7) or as a percentage of the page size. For example: **<img scr="polar bear.jpg width="379" height="262">** would make your picture fairly large. To make it appear across the middle of your page, add the tag **<p align=center>** just before your picture tag.

Webmonkey tutorials

These projects will get you started using HTML, but once you're feeling a little more confident, you can visit the **Webmonkey** site, which has some good HTML tutorials. It contains lots of new tags which you can use to add extra design features to your page, and there is a complete list of hex codes (see project 99).

101 • Put your page on the Web

When you have completed your Web page, you can put it onto the World Wide Web. This is called uploading. When you upload your page, millions of people will be able to see it, so make sure that you have read your page through carefully. Look for spelling mistakes, and make sure that all the information you've included is accurate. Also be aware that you may receive lots of junk e-mails (known as spam mail) if you post a personal e-mail address on your Web site.

Web sites are stored on powerful computers called servers, or hosts. In order to put your page on the World Wide Web, you'll need to rent some Web space on a server, and transfer your Web page on to it. The easiest way to do this is through your Internet Service Provider (see page 3). Lots of ISPs offer their customers free Web space. If yours doesn't, you may have to pay a small monthly fee for the space, or you could try using a different ISP.

The host will give you an official Web address (URL) for your site. To find out how to get a URL, visit your host's Web site and look for a link to instructions on how to get some Web space and how to set up a Web site. To transfer the Web page from your computer to the Web server, you will need to use a special program called an "FTP client". Your ISP should have details of how you can download one.

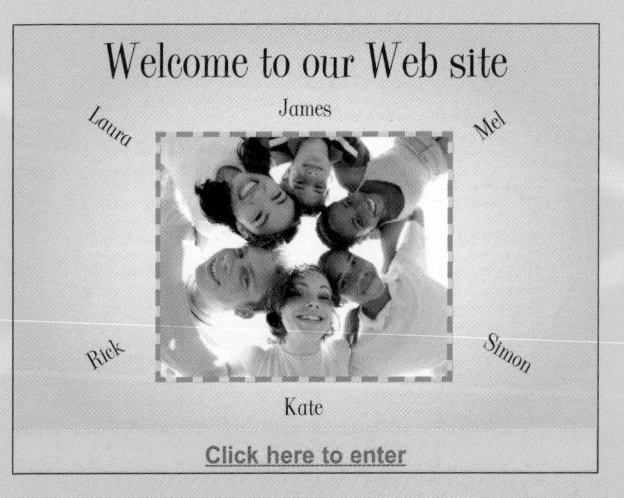

Safety

The Internet brings you access to millions of pages of information, as well as the ability to contact people anywhere in the world. This makes it an amazing resource, but it is also possible that you will come into contact with people, information and pictures that are unpleasant and even dangerous.

Make sure you follow the guidelines on this page, and throughout the book, so you don't put your safety at risk. The **Usborne Web site** has more information on staying safe on the Internet. Click on *Net help* on the home page.

Personal details

Never give out your personal details (especially your full name, address, and telephone number) over the Internet. This includes in e-mails, mailing lists, and especially during any form of online chat (see pages 14-17 for more information). The only exception to the rule is when you're paying for things online on a shopping site that uses a secure server (see the safety boxes on page 33).

Also be cautious about giving out your e-mail address to others. Lots of sites will ask you for it when you try to use certain areas of their Web site, or when you are downloading a program. If you give it out too freely, you'll start receiving hundreds of junk e-mails, known as "spam mail", which can become very annoying.

If a Web site does ask you for personal information, look for a "privacy policy" section on the site. This should include a promise that they will not give your details to anyone else.

Using filters

Everybody is free to publish their own Web pages and, unfortunately, this means that, as well as the millions of interesting sites, there are also lots of unpleasant and offensive ones.

It is possible to block most of these unsuitable sites, so you don't accidentally visit them while you're browsing the Internet. To do this you need a filter program. You'll find more about filter programs, and where to get the right one for you at the **GetNetWise Web site**.

Meeting people

You can't see what anyone looks like when you're communicating over the Internet. Because of this, some people pretend to be something that they're not. Just be aware of this, and never assume that anything someone says is necessarily true.

Chat rooms can be a common place for unpleasant characters to hang out. It is important that you always use monitored chat rooms (see pages 16-17), where conversations are monitored to prevent any inappropriate or offensive language. If someone does say something unpleasant to you while you're in a chat room, don't respond to them. Contact the site monitor and tell them about it.

Viruses

A computer virus is a program which attacks your computer's memory, and destroys information on it permanently. You can easily download a computer virus by accident when you download a program from the Internet, or when you open an e-mail attachment.

To protect your computer against viruses, you should install a virus shield. This is a special program which automatically checks any files you have downloaded before you open them. Most new computers come with a virus shield installed, but as there are new viruses appearing all the time, it is important that you update your software every few months.

If you already have one, you can do a keyword search, using your virus shield's name as a keyword, to find its official Web site. There, you should find details about the latest updates. If you don't already have one, you can download a demo version of the *McAfee VirusScan®* shield at the **McAfee Web site**.

Glossary

Here is a list of Internet and computer words you may come across while you are using this book. Some of these words have more than one meaning. The definitions here are the ones which apply to the Internet. Any word which appears in *italic* type is defined elsewhere in the glossary.

applet A tiny program written in a programming language called *Java*™ .
bit The smallest amount of computer data.
bookmark Netscape Navigator's way of creating a short cut to a *URL*, so you can find it again easily.
bps or **bits per second** The unit used to measure how fast data is transferred between two computers.
browser A piece of *software* which finds and displays *Web pages*.
browsing Exploring sites on the *Internet*.
byte A unit of eight *bit*s
chat room A *Web site* where *Internet* users can chat to each other.
client A computer which uses the services of a *host* or *server* computer
clip art *Digital* pictures, which are often free from copyright, and can be used to decorate documents.
compressing Making a smaller version of a *file*, so that it takes up less space in your computer's memory and less time to *download*.
demo A trial version of a game or program which is free to *download*.
dialog box A box which appears on the screen to display, or request, information. It will disappear after you enter the information.
digital Information recorded as a number code that can be read and processed by a computer.
directory A *search engine* that organizes *Web pages* into categories which you can *browse*.
domain name The part of a *URL* which gives information about what type of organization the site belongs to, or where it is located.
download To copy *files*, such as *Web pages* or programs, onto your computer.
dpi or **dots per inch** Measurement of how clear a picture will appear when it has been converted into computer data using a *scanner*.
drop-down menu or **pull-down menu** A list of options that appears on the screen when you click on its title.
eCash® Computer data with the same value as paper and metal money.
e-mail A way of sending text messages from one computer to another.
emoticon or **smiley** A picture, which looks like a face, made of keyboard characters.
encryption Turning private information into a special code, so that nobody else can read it while it travels across the *Internet*.
e-zine A magazine which is published on a Web site, instead of in paper form.
FAQs or **Frequently Asked Questions** The answers to questions most often asked by visitors to a *Web site*.
favorite Internet Explorer's way of creating a short cut to a *URL*, so you can easily find it.
file Anything stored on a computer, such as a document, image or a program.
file format The way a *file* is stored so that it can be used with a particular program.
filter A program which checks *Web pages* and *e-mail*s, then blocks any unpleasant content.
FTP or **File Transfer Protocol** The system used to transfer *files* between computers over the *Internet*.
GIF A *file format* used to save *graphics* for use on *Web pages*.
graphics Pictures created using a computer.
hardware The equipment that makes up a computer or a *network*.
hex code A code system in *HTML,* used to add different shades to a page. Each shade has its own special hex code.
home page An introductory Web page which contains *links* to other pages on a *Web site*.
host A computer connected to the *Internet* which holds information that can be accessed by other *Internet* users.
HTML or **HyperText Mark-Up Language** The computer code used to create *Web pages*.
hyperlink or **link** A piece of text or a picture which you click on to link from one *Web page* to another.
icon A symbol on the screen representing an application or a piece of data.

interactive A Web site containing features which you can respond to or change.
Internet The worldwide computer *network* which is made up of many smaller networks.
Internet Service Provider or **ISP** also known as an **Internet Access Provider** or **IAP** A company offering people *Internet* connections.
Java™ A programming language used to add *interactive* features to *Web pages*.
JPEG A *file format* used to save photographs for use on *Web pages*.
KB or **kilobyte** A unit of approximately 1,000 *bytes*.
keyword Any word that you ask a *search engine* to look for.
link See *hyperlinks*.
mailing list A discussion group where group members receive messages by *e-mail*.
MB or **megabyte** A unit of one million *bytes*.
modem A device that allows computer data to be sent down a telephone line.
monitored chat room or **moderated chat room** A *chat room* where conversations are monitored by people to make sure that there are no offensive or inappropriate discussions.
MP3 A *file format* for music clips which takes up very little memory space.
multimedia A combination of *graphics*, sound and animation.
network A number of computers and other devices that are linked together, so that they can share information and equipment.
offline Not connected to the *Internet*.
online Connected to the *Internet*.
online form Item on a *Web page* which you can fill out to send information over the *Internet*.
pixels or **picture elements** The dots which make up the pictures you see on your computer screen.
plug-in A piece of *software* you can add to your *browser* to enable it to perform extra functions, such as displaying video clips.
portal A *Web site* which has lots of *links*.
RAM or **Random Access Memory** The largest part of your computer's memory, where information is stored.
resolution The number of *pixels* which make up the picture you see on screen. The higher the resolution, the sharper the picture.
scanner A device used to make a *digital* copy of a picture so that a computer can read it.
search engine A program which searches for *Web pages* which contain particular words.
secure server A computer which handles *encrypted* information, such as financial information, so that nobody else can read it.
serial port A socket on a computer through which a *modem* can be connected.
server A computer which connects individual computers to the *Internet*.
software Programs that enable computers to carry out certain tasks.
subscribe To add your name to a *mailing list*.
tag An *HTML* instruction.
thumbnail A small picture shown on a *Web page*, which you can click on to see a larger version.
unsubscribe To cancel a subscription to a *mailing list*.
upload To copy *files*, over the *Internet*, from your computer to another computer.
URL or **Uniform Resource Locator** or **Universal Resource Locator** The specific address of a *Web page*.
virus A program which interrupts the normal functioning of your *hardware* or *software*.
wallpaper The background display on your computer's desktop.
Web camera or **Webcam** A camera which transmits live images over the *Internet* via a computer.
Web editor A program which lets you create a *Web page* without knowing *HTML* code.
Web page A computer document written in *HTML* and linked to other pages by *hyperlinks*.
Web site A collection of *Web pages* set up by an organization or an individual.
Web space The computer space *ISPs* make available for people to create their own Web sites.
World Wide Web or **Web** A huge collection of information available on the *Internet*. The information is divided up into *Web pages* which are joined together by *hyperlinks*.
zip file A *file* which has been *compressed*.

Index

Acknowledgements

Every effort has been made to trace the copyright holders of the material in this book. If any rights have been omittted, the publishers offer their sincere apologies and will rectify this in any subsequent editions following notification.

Screen shots used with permission from Microsoft Corporation. QuickTime is a trademark of Apple Computers, Inc., registered in the US and other countries. Flash and Shockwave are trademarks of Macromedia, Inc., registered in the US and other countries.

Cover: UFO image © Corbis Stock Market; Satellite pictures of tropical storms from the NASA – Earth Science Enterprise site; Tyrannosaurus artwork by Joe Tucciarone; Weather map from the NCDC Climate Visualization site.

p2-3 Tooncar screenshots © Copyright 2001, LifeLine Entertainment (also on p4 and 24); Mythweb screenshot © Mythweb (also on p46); British Museum screenshot © Copyright The British Museum (also on p48-49); The Tech Museum of Innovation, San Jose, CA, USA www.thetech.org screenshot used with permission; With thanks to the FC Barcelona Web site (also on p23); Aboriginal Art online screenshot © www.aboriginal artonline.com; Amusement Park Physics based on "The Mechanical Universe" – Annenberg/CPB (also on p44); Landscape photo: Digital Vision.

p4-5 Web site for the Royal College of Art, created by Deepend, London 1999; Le musée de la musique Web site graphic conception : Cité de la musique / Dan Benesch; With thanks to FNAC (also on p30) and the BBC Weather Centre (also on p55); Pixar screenshot Copyright © 2001 Pixar Animation Studios.

p6-7 www.TryScience.org TryScience/New York Hall of Science. With thanks to Canon for images of the S630 Bubble Jet printer and CanoScan N676U; With thanks to Gateway for the image of a Gateway Performance PC and Hewlett Packard/Beattie Media for the image of an hp photosmart c200 digital camera.

p8-9 © BrainPOP 2001. All rights reserved (also on p44); Shrek Web site image courtesy of PDI/DreamWorks, © 2001; Google Brand features are trademarks of Google, Inc; Yahoo!, the Yahoo! logo, Yahooligans!, the Yahooligans! design are trademarks of Yahoo! Inc. (also on pg 10-11 and 16); With thanks to Lycos UK Ltd, Ask Jeeves!, Excite, The Microsoft Network (MSN) and KidsClick! – The Web search for kids by librarians; AltaVista © 2001 AltaVista Company. All Rights Reserved (also on pg 11); With thanks to the Center for Captive Chimpanzee Care.

p10-11 The Simpsons Web site © FOX and its related entities. All rights reserved.

p12-13 Marcelle the cow images © Phong for Bechamel.com Copyright 1991-2001 WinZip Computing, Inc. WinZip® is a registered trademark of WinZip Computing, Inc.; WinZip is available from www.winzip.com WinZip screen images reproduced with permission of WinZip Computing, Inc.

p14-15 E-card © Kersten Brothers Studios.

p18-19 PDI/Dreamworks Web site image courtesy of PDI/DreamWorks, © 2001; Scooby Doo screenshot © 2001 – Warner Brothers – All Rights Reserved. HARRYPOTTER, characters, names and related indicia and WARNER BROS., shield logo and related indicia are trademarks of Warner Bros. TM & © 2001.

p20-21 NME.com and Rockstar.it screenshots used with permission; With thanks to dotmusic.com Ltd. and Turntables; RealPlayer, RealJukeBox and Surreal FX Design are the registered trademarks of RealNetworks, Inc. registered in the US and other countries.

p22-23 Wrestlers: Digital Vision; With thanks to the International Olympics Committee (IOC) and SportsID.

p24-25 AquaNox © Massive Development GmbH; Virtual Pool 2 courtesy of Interplay Productions Ltd; Amped: Freestyle screenshot © 2001 Microsoft Corporation. All rights reserved; EverQuest is a registered trademark of Sony Computer Entertainment America Inc. © 1999-2001 Sony Computer Entertainment America Inc. All rights reserved; Sierra and the "S" logo are trademarks of Sierra On-Line, Inc. NASCAR® is a registered trademark of the National Association for Stock Car Auto Racing, Inc.

p26-27 Landscape, koala, flower, giraffe and group pictures: Digital Vision; Picture of Mandela supplied by Hector Goransky.

p28-29 BBC Food screenshot reproduced with the permission of the BBC © 2001; With thanks to Howard Allman and Leaping Salmon; Fresh Starts screenshot copyright © 1998 BASF Corporation, used with the permission of BASF Corporation; Hamburger image © White Castle System, Inc. used with permission.

p30-31 "Today is lemonade" animated poem: Ingrid Ankerson © 2000-2001 All Rights Reserved; BBC Poetry and animated history of books screenshots c/o BBC Arts. Writers' Window screenshot reproduced with the permission of UNITEC in Schools (http://schools.unitecnology. ac.nz) and English Online (http://english.unitecnology.ac.nz). All content added by visitors to the site is moderated on a daily basis. Amazon.co.uk is a trademark of Amazon .com, Inc. in the U.S. and/or other countries; Achuka screenshot used with permission www.achuka.co.uk; Use of artwork and materials from www.roalddahl.com (c RDNL) by kind permission of Dahl and Dahl; With thanks to Ian McNee, FNAC and Ricochet – The European Portal to Children's Literature.

p32-33 With thanks to Interflora, VirtualMarket.it, Godiva and La Redoute; eCash and the eCash logo are registered trademarks of eCash technologies, Inc. © 2000, 2001 eCash Technologies, Inc. All Rights reserved. With thanks to Haburi.

p34-35 Dog photos: copyright Diane Miller 2000. Mountain Lion: Digital Vision. With thanks to National Geographic/Monterey Bay Aquarium, and eNature. Bird in flight image Tom Vezo/Herbert Clark. Zebra picture: Siobhan Williams.

p36-37 Panda Passport Web site © WWF International; The WWF Virtual House was reprinted with permission from World Wildlife Fund, © 1999, 2000, 2001; With thanks to Greenpeace and Greenpeace Belgium.

p38-39 Star Tribune homework help screenshot copyright 2001 Star Tribune. Republished with permission; Images from the clip art gallery on Discovery School.com used with permission; With thanks to Big Chalk.

p40-41 With thanks to the National Aeronautics and Space Administration (NASA) Office of Space Science; Saturn picture: Taken on January 4 1998. Hubble Space Telescope NICMOS Image credit: Erich Karkoschka (University of Arizona), and NASA; Crab Nebula picture: J Hester and P. Scowen (Arizona State Univ.), and NASA; Gamma Ray Bursts: Digital Vision; Virtual Space Tour™ copyright 2000 SPACE.COM.

p42-43 With thanks to Gelios Software www.gelio soft.com and Horizon Originals – Horizon reserves the right for design and Image of Horizon Originals dinosaur series; Dinosaur simulation screen shots reproduced by permission from Donald Henderson. Thanks to the Smithsonian National Museum of Natural History; The Cave of Lascaux Web site © Ministry of Culture and Communication/Texts, Photographs and Illustrations Norbert Aujoulat © National Centre of Prehistory.

p44-45 Why Files – Copyright, University of Wisconzin Board of Regents; Visual Elements Periodic Table © Murray Robertson 1998-1999.

p46-47 The Pyramids at Giza, Egypt © Charles & Josette Lenars/CORBIS; Family photos: Bruce Ruiz at www.Bruce.Ruiz.net; Thanks to the Musée de la Tapisserie.

p48-49 With thanks to the State Hermitage Museum, St Petersburg; Copyright ©2001 State Hermitage Museum. Reproduced picture: Still life with apples, Paul Cezanne, 1908; The Museum of Modern Art, Web site: www.moma.org © 2001 The Museum of Modern Art, New York. The Museum of Modern Art, Web site: ww.moma.org/onlineprojects/artsafari/ safari_sleeping.html © 1999 The Museum of Modern Art, New York. Art Direction: Greg Van Alstyne, The Museum of Modern Art; Design and Programming: OVEN, New York. Monet at Giverny : Masterpieces from the Musée Marmottan, presented at the Montreal Museum of Fine Arts from January 28 to May 9, 1999. Photo: Courtesy of The Montreal Museum of Fine Arts; With thanks to Chelsea Isbister of Saskatoon, SK Canada and Nevena Vereski.

p50-51 © Pariscope.fr The Pariscope web site is published and maintained by LHFI, 11 rue de Cambrai, 75019 Paris, France. All rights reserved. Copyright 2001; With thanks to Time Out. WOMAD screenshot © Real World Holdings Ltd; Train Picture: Digital Vision; Maporama screenshots used with permission.

p52-53 One World Journeys screenshot © OneWorldJourneys.com; Air France screenshot copyright © AIR FRANCE 2001; With thanks to FunAdventure.com and American Express.

p54-55 © Ananova Ltd. 2001. Reproduced by permission. All rights reserved. With thanks to La Stampa, AFP and abc news.com

p56-57 With thanks to Rowena Dugdale www.rowenadugdale.com Collage and Montage illustration and Slam America.

p58-59 Group photos: Digital Vision.

First published in 2002 by Usborne Publishing Ltd., Usborne House, 83-85 Saffron Hill, London EC1N 8RT, England. www.usborne.com.